Student Lab Manual to Accompany

HEALTH ASSESSMENT & PHYSICAL EXAMINATION

Third Edition

Mary Ellen Zator Estes,
RN, MSN, FNP, APRN-BC, NP-C
Family Nurse Practitioner
in Internal Medicine
Fairfax, Virginia
and
Clinical Faculty, Nurse Pracitioner Track
School of Nursing
Ball State University
Muncie, Indiana

Prepared by
Kathleen Peck Schaefer, RNC, MSN, MEd
Assistant Professor of Nursing
School of Health Professions
Marymount University
Arlington, Virginia
and
Nursing Staff
Inova Fairfax Hospital
Falls Church, Virginia

THOMSON

DELMAR LEARNING

Australia   Canada   Mexico   Singapore   Spain   United Kingdom   United States

THOMSON

DELMAR LEARNING

Student Lab Manual to Accompany Health Assessment and Physical Examination, Third Edition
by Mary Ellen Zator Estes

Vice President, Health Care Business Unit:
William Brottmiller

Editorial Director:
Cathy L. Esperti

Executive Editor:
Matthew Kane

Editorial Assistant:
Tiffiny Adams

Marketing Director:
Jennifer McAvey

Marketing Coordinator:
Michele Gleason

Technology Project Manager:
Mary Colleen Liburdi

Technology Project Coordinator:
Carolyn Fox

Assistant to Production and Technology Directors
Kate Kaufman

Production Director:
Carolyn Miller

Art and Design Specialist:
Robert Plante

Production Coordinator:
Mary Ellen Cox

Senior Project Editor:
David Buddle

Notice to the Reader

Contents

Preface

This lab manual is designed to accompany *Health Assessment & Physical Examination,* third edition, by Mary Ellen Zator Estes. Each of the 25 chapters in this lab manual is developed to facilitate student learning of health assessment skills in a varied format. By using this lab manual at home and in the laboratory setting, nursing students will work with important concepts and begin to apply them to real-life situations.

As a clinical/lab instructor, I have developed guides and quizzes to help students grasp the concepts and procedures in clinical nursing. The nursing laboratory can and should be a center of dynamic instruction and learning. Enthusiastic and creative instructors, provided with resources that include well-developed laboratory guides, help students acquire the skills needed for competent and compassionate nursing care. As the patient population becomes increasingly diverse and ill, the nurse's health assessment skills become more essential, and the use of a lab manual to enhance student learning gains importance. This lab manual provides a guide for that learning.

Lab Practice for Critical Thinking and the Nursing Process

Chapter

1

Learning Objectives

1. Relate critical thinking skills to nursing practice.
2. Identify the phases of the nursing process.
3. Compare nursing care plans and critical pathways.

Reading Assignment

Before beginning this lab assignment, please read Chapter 1, Critical Thinking and the Nursing Process, in *Health Assessment & Physical Examination* (3rd ed.) by Mary Ellen Zator Estes.

Key Terms

Please define the following terms:

actual nursing diagnosis_____

_____

assessment_____

_____

clinical reasoning _____

_____

clustering _____

_____

collaborative interventions _____

_____

collaborative problem _____

_____

critical pathway _____

_____

critical thinking _____

_____

defining characteristics _____

_____

descriptor _____

_____

evaluation _____
_____

evidence-based practice_____
_____

Functional Health Patterns _____
_____

Human Response Patterns_____
_____

implementation _____
_____

independent nursing interventions _____
_____

intervention _____
_____

long-term outcome_____
_____

NANDA _____
_____

nursing care plan _____
_____

nursing diagnosis _____
_____

nursing process _____
_____

objective data _____
_____

outcomes identification _____
_____

patient goal _____
_____

patient outcome _____
_____

PES method_____
_____

planning _____
_____

prioritize _____
_____

qualifier _____
_____

related factors _____

_____

risk nursing diagnosis_____

_____

short-term outcome _____

_____

subjective data _____

_____

taxonomy _____

_____

wellness nursing diagnosis _____

_____

Laboratory Activities

1. What is the role of critical thinking in your practice as a nurse?

_____

_____

_____

_____

_____

2. Identify the seven Universal Intellectual Standards for critical thinking.

A. _____   E. _____

B. _____   F. _____

C. _____   G. _____

D. _____

3. You have just accepted a new position on a critical care unit and are eager to improve your clinical reasoning skills. What activities can help you achieve this goal?

_____

_____

_____

_____

4. List specific ways that critical thinking will enhance your health assessment skills.

_____

_____

_____

_____

_____

5. Describe and define the *nursing process.*

_____
_____
_____
_____

6. What information is collected in the *assessment* phase of the nursing process?

_____
_____
_____
_____
_____

7. Compare the approach of the body system assessment with the Functional Health Patterns assessment. Which approach is cephalocaudal?

_____
_____
_____
_____
_____

8. List five common errors in writing nursing diagnoses.

   A. _____
   B. _____
   C. _____
   D. _____
   E. _____

9. What steps are involved in the *planning* phase of the nursing process? Why should the patient be involved in this phase?

_____
_____
_____
_____

10. What nursing actions are involved in the *implementation* phase of the nursing process?

_____
_____
_____
_____

11. How do critical pathways compare with the nursing care plan? Does evaluation differ in the two processes?

    _____

    _____

    _____

    _____

12. What is the impact of evidence-based practice on health care?

    _____

    _____

    _____

Self-Assessment Quiz

1. What are the six phases of the nursing process?

    A. _____

    B. _____

    C. _____

    D. _____

    E. _____

    F. _____

2. Match each of the following to the phase of the nursing process in which it occurs:

    _____ Patient's progress toward outcomes is determined   **A** Assessment

    _____ Time frame varies with each patient   **D** Nursing Diagnosis

    _____ Nursing database   **O** Outcome Identification

    _____ Prioritization of nursing diagnoses

    _____ Information based on Functional Health Patterns   **P** Planning

    _____ Patient goals   **I** Implementation

    _____ Helps patient meet predetermined outcomes   **E** Evaluation

    _____ May review factors preventing goal achievement

    _____ Clinical judgment about patient responses to health problems

3. True or false?

    ☐ **T** ☐ **F**   Maslow's Hierarchy of Needs could be used to prioritize interventions.

    ☐ **T** ☐ **F**   Critical pathways are based on the patient's Diagnostic-Related Grouping.

    ☐ **T** ☐ **F**   Short-term and long-term outcomes are included for every patient outcome.

    ☐ **T** ☐ **F**   Patient goals should be well-defined with measurable outcomes.

    ☐ **T** ☐ **F**   Nursing diagnoses are usually excluded from critical pathways.

    ☐ **T** ☐ **F**   Collaborative interventions utilize resources from departments other than nursing.

4. Which of the following nursing diagnoses are written incorrectly?

    A. Impaired adjustment related to necessity for major lifestyle change.

    B. Hyperemesis gravidarum related to abnormal fluid loss secondary to vomiting.

    C. Risk for injury related to altered clotting factors.

    D. Altered nutrition, more than body requirements, related to eating too much.

5. The _____ combines the elements of the nursing process to document the progress of patient care in a standardized fashion.

Lab Practice for the Patient Interview

Learning Objectives

1. Identify effective interviewing techniques.
2. Conduct a patient interview.
3. Review characteristics of nontherapeutic and problematic interviewing techniques.
4. Identify interviewing techniques used with special populations.

Reading Assignment

Before beginning this lab assignment, please read Chapter 2, The Patient Interview, in *Health Assessment & Physical Examination* (3rd ed.) by Mary Ellen Zator Estes.

Key Terms

Please define the following terms:

action response _____

_____

active listening _____

_____

colloquialism _____

_____

intermediary _____

_____

HIPAA _____

_____

joining stage _____

_____

listening response _____

_____

nonverbal communication _____

_____

termination stage _____

_____

working stage _____

_____

Laboratory Activities

1. What types of information are collected during the patient interview?

   _____

   _____

   _____

   _____

   _____

2. How is the patient an active participant in the interview process?

   _____

   _____

   _____

   _____

3. Describe what occurs in each stage of the interview process:

   Stage I: *Joining* _____

   Stage II: *Working* _____

   Stage III: *Termination* _____

4. What role can family members or caregivers play during the interview process?

   _____

   _____

   _____

5. Give five examples of nonverbal cues that the nurse may observe.

   A. _____

   B. _____

   C. _____

   D. _____

   E. _____

6. Contrast listening responses and action responses in the patient interview.

   _____

   _____

   _____

   _____

   _____

7. What is *social distance* and why is it usually appropriate for interviewing a patient?

_____

_____

_____

8. Give an example for each of these effective questioning and listening response techniques:

Open-ended question_____

Closed question _____

Making observations _____

Restating _____

Reflecting _____

Clarifying_____

Sequencing _____

Encouraging comparisons _____

Summarizing _____

How can silence be an effective tool?

_____

_____

_____

_____

9. What nontherapeutic interviewing technique does each of the following statements represent? Rewrite each for a more appropriate statement.

A. "Why did you get pregnant again so soon?"

_____

_____

B. "You don't want to take more pain medicine yet, do you?"

_____

_____

C. "You won't have any trouble doing this dressing change at home."

_____

_____

D. "If I were you, I'd definitely have that lump removed."

_____

_____

10. Contrast each of the following pairs of effective and ineffective techniques:

Exploring vs. probing _____ , _____
_____
_____

Informing vs. advising _____
_____
_____

Normalizing vs. false reassurance _____
_____
_____

Limit setting vs. interrupting _____
_____
_____

Presenting reality vs. defending_____
_____
_____

11. What strategies may be helpful when confronted with a hostile patient?
_____
_____
_____
_____

Signs of increasing tension in the patient may include:
_____
_____
_____

12. List three strategies to facilitate interviewing patients with each of the following special needs:

Hearing-impaired _____
_____
_____

Visually impaired _____
_____
_____

Aphasic _____
_____
_____

Non-English-speaking_____
_____
_____

Older adult _____

_____

_____

Self-Assessment Quiz

1. _____, or the act of perceiving what is said both verbally and nonverbally, is a critical factor in conducting a successful health assessment interview.

2. Identify five problematic questioning techniques.

   A. _____

   B. _____

   C. _____

   D. _____

   E. _____

3. True or false?

   ☐ **T** ☐ **F** Speaking more loudly and slowly to a patient who lip-reads is helpful.

   ☐ **T** ☐ **F** *Social distance* allows good eye contact.

   ☐ **T** ☐ **F** Closed questions are best to use with a patient who has aphasia.

   ☐ **T** ☐ **F** Ask permission before touching a patient who has visual impairment.

   ☐ **T** ☐ **F** "You don't drink, do you?" is an example of *probing*.

4. Which technique is used for each of the following statements?

reflecting	collaborating
confronting	informing
normalizing	focusing
exploring	encouraging comparisons

   _____ A. "Tell me more about the symptoms you experienced yesterday."

   _____ B. "You sound upset about that."

   _____ C. "You talked about your problems following the diet. Let's talk a little more about that."

   _____ D. "Have you had this type of headache before?"

   _____ E. "Many patients have the same concerns you do about this type of treatment."

5. Techniques to handle a sexually aggressive patient include:

_____

_____

_____

Lab Practice for the Complete Health History Including Documentation

Chapter 3

Learning Objectives

1. Identify the components of a complete health history.
2. Complete a history of present illness (HPI) for a chief complaint.
3. Draw a genogram to illustrate a family health history.
4. Conduct a review of systems (ROS).
5. Review documentation guidelines.

Reading Assignment

Before beginning this lab assignment, please read Chapter 3, The Complete Health History Including Documentation, in *Health Assessment & Physical Examination* (3rd ed.) by Mary Ellen Zator Estes.

Key Terms

Please define the following terms:

aggravating factors _____

_____

alleviating factors _____

_____

associated manifestations _____

_____

cephalocaudal _____

_____

characteristic patterns of daily living _____

_____

chief complaint _____

_____

complete health history _____

_____

distress _____

_____

emergency health history _____

_____

episodic health history _____

_____

eustress _____

_____

follow-up health history_____

_____

functional health assessment _____

_____

genogram_____

_____

genomics _____

_____

health maintenance activities _____

_____

history of the present illness _____

_____

interval health history _____

_____

pack/year history _____

_____

past health history _____

_____

patient profile _____

_____

pertinent negatives_____

_____

reason for seeking health care_____

_____

review of systems _____

_____

sequelae_____

_____

sign_____

_____

social history_____

_____

stress _____

_____

symptom _____

_____

Visual Analog Scale _____

_____

Laboratory Activities

1. What are the purposes of a written health history? Why is the health history interview usually completed before the physical assessment?

   _____

   _____

   _____

   _____

   _____

2. In what situations might the source of the information be someone other than the patient?

   _____

   _____

   _____

3. Which diseases would be noted in the communicable disease section?

   _____

   _____

   _____

   Which diseases can be included in the childhood illnesses section?

   _____

   _____

   _____

4. What are the 10 characteristics of a chief complaint that should be included for a complete history of present illness?

   A. _____

   B. _____

   C. _____

   D. _____

   E. _____

   F. _____

   G. _____

   H. _____

   I. _____

   J. _____

   Suggest ways a patient could describe the severity of a symptom.

   _____

   _____

   _____

   _____

5. List five questions that you might ask a patient for the ROS for each of the following:

Skin

A. _____

B. _____

C. _____

D. _____

E. _____

Cardiovascular

A. _____

B. _____

C. _____

D. _____

E. _____

Musculoskeletal

A. _____

B. _____

C. _____

D. _____

E. _____

Female/Male Reproductive

A. _____

B. _____

C. _____

D. _____

E. _____

6. You will now be conducting the first part of the health and physical assessment. Conduct a complete health history for the following information:

Identifying Information

Today's Date   January 15, 2008

Biographical Data

Patient's Name   Mrs. Smith

Address   123 County Rd. 20

Phone Number   519-987-6543

Date of Birth   August 10, 1913

Birthplace   England

Social Security Number   135 846 216

Occupation	Retired
Work Address	N/A
Insurance	West Life
Usual Source of Health Care	Walk-in Clinic & Pharmacy
Source of Referral	Dr. Laing
Emergency Contact	Daughter (Rose)

**Source and Reliability
of Information**

Son (Ronald)

Patient Profile

Age	95
Gender	Female
Race	Caucasian
Marital Status	Widowed

**Reason for Seeking Health Care
or Chief Complaint**

Possible broken hip
(Slip and fall accident)

**Present Health or
History of Present Illness**

Location	hip and upper limb
Radiation	down leg
Quality	Severe
Quantity	constant
Associated Manifestations	sore ribs
Aggravating Factors	scrape on side of abdomen
Alleviating Factors	laying on opposite side
Setting	icy steps
Timing	early morning while getting mail
Meaning and Impact	Slipped on step and fell
	down steps onto hip

Past Health History

Medical History

Breast Cancer
Type 2 diabetes

Surgical History

pt. had right breast removed
in 1980

Medications
  Prescription   insulin dependent
                     Blood pressure medication

  OTC   Aspirin

  General Questions pt. questions cholesteral levels
  Communicable Diseases

  Allergies   peanuts and bee stings
  Injuries/Accidents broke wrist last fall

  Special Needs   Constant reminding to check sugar
  Blood Transfusions N/A
  Childhood Illnesses mumps

  Immunizations   polio, flu shot

Construct a genogram using information from the family health history. Try to include the grandparents and any aunts and uncles. Add abbreviations to the legend as needed.

LEGEND
◯ Living female
▢ Living male
● or ⊗ Deceased female
■ or ☒ Deceased male
╱ Points to patient
Female twins
Male twins
—//— Divorced
A&W = Alive & well
CA = Cancer
HTN = Hypertension

Family Health History

History of heart disease & colon cancer

Social History

Alcohol Use

recovered alcoholic

Drug Use

N/A

Tobacco Use

1 pack/day - 50 yrs

Domestic and Intimate
   Partner Violence

N/A

Sexual Practice

Widowed since 1990

Travel History

hasn't travelled in 20 yrs

Work Environment

N/A - Retired

Home Environment
   Physical Environment

lives at home - children look after her daily

   Psychosocial Environment

likes to knitt and watch

Hobbies and Leisure Activities

oprah

Stress

moderate

Education

high school diploma

Economic Status

middle class

Military Service

N/A

Religion

Catholic

Ethnic Background

Canadian

Roles and Relationships

mother of 2 - grandmother

Characteristic Patterns of
   Daily Living and Functional
   Health Assessment

-should not be left along
-risk for falls and improper care of diabetes
- doesn't get proper nutrition
- consider long term care

Health Maintenance Activities

Sleep

Sleeps periodically through day

Diet

poor eating habits

Exercise

N/A

Stress Management

N/A

Use of Safety Devices	N/A
Health Check-ups	doesn't like to go to doctors children take her sometimes

Review of Systems

General	Slightly overweight
Skin	dry, wrinkles
Hair	grey, dry
Nails	yellowed, brittle
Eyes	a bit cloudy, uses glasses
Ears	poor hearing in both ears
Nose and Sinuses	poor sense of smell
Mouth	moist, dentures
Throat and Neck	swollen glands
Respiratory	trouble breathing
Cardiovascular	heart murmer
Breasts and Axilla	missing rt. breast
Gastrointestinal	N/A
Urinary	bladder infection
Musculoskeletal	N/A
Neurological	memory problems
Psychological	misses husband — Rodger

Female or Male Reproductive	Female
Nutrition	poor – hardly eats
Endocrine	
Lymph Nodes	Swollen
Hematological	

7. How can you deal with sensitive topics such as alcohol use, drug use, or sexual practices during the health history interview?

_____

_____

_____

_____

_____

8. List the documentation guidelines for assessment-specific information.

_____

_____

_____

_____

_____

_____

_____

_____

9. What is wrong with each of the following charted statements?

A. Lump in outer quadrant of left breast feels smaller today.

_____

_____

_____

B. Patient uncooperative during neuro exam.

_____

_____

C. Complaining of pain occasionally in the right arm.

_____

_____

_____

D. Large abrasion noted on upper abdomen

_____

_____

_____

E. *nl cap refill*

_____

_____

_____

10. What clues would alert you to possible domestic or intimate partner violence?

_____

_____

_____

Self-Assessment Quiz

1. What are the four types of health history?
   A. Complete
   B. episodic
   C. interval or follow-up
   D. emergency

2. In which section of the health history would each of these items be documented?

   E Denies hx of hepatitis, AIDS   A. Biographical Data

   G Works long hours at stressful job   B. Patient Profile

   I Denies change in moles

   G College graduate   C. Chief Complaint

   A Husband is emergency contact   D. History of Present Illness

   B Asian   E. Past Health History

   D Felt "well" until 2 days ago   F. Family Health History

   F Sibling died in skiing accident

   C "I have an itchy rash on my legs."   G. Social History

   H Sleeps 7 hours a night, feels rested.   H. Health Maintenance Activities

   I Blood type "O negative"   I. Review of Systems

3. True or false?

   ☐ T ☑ F   Terms such as *burning*, *stabbing*, and *aching* describe the quantity of pain.

   ☑ T ☐ F   A *sign* is an objective finding; a *symptom* is a subjective finding.

   ☑ T ☐ F   Information on the setting for a CC can include the patient's mental state.

   ☐ T ☑ F   Information on exposure to communicable diseases is usually limited to the last 10 years.

   ☐ T ☑ F   Questions about sexual practice should be omitted on the patient's first visit.

   ☑ T ☐ F   The ROS usually follows a cephalocaudal approach.

   ☐ T ☑ F   The CAGE questionnaire is a screening tool for drug abuse.

   ☐ T ☑ F   Correct another person's entry only if you know the information is false.

   ☐ T ☑ F   If possible, avoid abbreviations when documenting patient information.

4. "What's missing from this picture?" Read this HPI in the patient's own words, and decide which of the ten characteristics of a chief complaint are missing.

   CC: *"I have a swollen ankle."*

   HPI: *"About three weeks ago, I hurt my left ankle on the edge of a chair and it's been swollen and sore off and on since then. It starts to ache if I walk too far at one time, or if I try to jog on it, so I've given that up for now. I tried sports tape wrapped around it, and that helped, but I'm just getting tired of having it like this. I'm worried that this could be arthritis like my mother has."*

   The missing characteristics are: _____

   _____

5. Draw a genogram using the following information. (Add any abbreviations used in the genogram to the legend.)

   Patient is female, married, 21 years old, and has mild asthma.

   Her husband is 23 and alive and well.

   They have a 2-year-old son who is a little obnoxious, but alive and well.

   Her parents are both 49 years old, divorced. Her father has hypertension and her mother has migraine headaches.

   She has two brothers, a 26-year-old who is alive and well and one who died in a motor vehicle accident at the age of 19.

   Her maternal grandparents include her 75-year-old grandmother, with congestive heart failure, and her grandfather, who died at the age of 68 of a myocardial infarction.

   There is no information on her paternal grandparents or any aunts or uncles.

LEGEND

◯ Living female

▢ Living male

● or ⊗ Deceased female

■ or ⊠ Deceased male

╱ Points to patient

─╫─ Divorced

A&W = Alive & well

CA = Cancer

HTN = Hypertension

6. Write a broad question that can be used to screen for domestic or intimate partner violence.

_____

_____

Lab Practice for Developmental Assessment

Learning Objectives

1. Compare theories of growth and development.
2. Describe developmental assessment tools.
3. Conduct developmental assessments on patients of different ages.

Reading Assignment

Before beginning this lab assignment, please read Chapter 4, Developmental Assessment, in *Health Assessment & Physical Examination* (3rd ed.) by Mary Ellen Zator Estes.

Key Terms

Please define the following terms:

ages and stages developmental theories_____

_____

castration anxiety _____

_____

conservation _____

_____

development_____

_____

developmental stage_____

_____

developmental task _____

_____

ego _____

_____

egocentrism _____

_____

Electra complex _____

_____

growth_____

_____

id _____
_____

life event theories_____
_____

life review _____
_____

object permanence _____
_____

Oedipus complex _____
_____

penis envy_____
_____

reversibility _____
_____

superego _____
_____

transitional development theories _____
_____

Laboratory Activities

1. Differentiate growth from development.
_____
_____
_____
_____
_____

2. Compare the ages and stages theory of development with the life events/transitional theory.
_____
_____
_____
_____
_____
_____

   Name four theorists who have generated ages and stages development theories.
   A. _____
   B. _____
   C. _____
   D. _____

3. What are cognitive life skills in Piaget's theory of cognitive development?

_____

_____

_____

_____

_____

List the four stages of Piaget's theory of development and the major tasks of each.

Developmental Stage and Age	Major Tasks

4. Differentiate the concepts of the id, the ego, and the superego according to Freud.

_____

_____

_____

_____

_____

5. Identify the age and major conflicts for each of Freud's psychosexual stages of development.

Stage	Age Range	Major Conflicts
Oral		
Anal		
Phallic		
Latency		
Genital		

6. List the eight stages (with approximate age) in Erikson's theory of personality development.

   A. _____

   B. _____

   C. _____

   D. _____

   E. _____

   F. _____

   G. _____

   H. _____

   How do individuals progress from one stage to the next?

   _____

   _____

   _____

   _____

   What stage do you feel is correlated with your own development, and why?

   _____

   _____

   _____

7. What are the three levels of Kohlberg's theory of moral development?

   A. _____

   _____

   _____

   B. _____

   _____

   _____

   C. _____

   _____

   _____

8. Compare the following theorists' views of the stages of development for an individual at ages 5, 15, and 25:

	Age 5	Age 15	Age 25
Freud			
Piaget			

	Age 5	Age 15	Age 25
Erikson			
Kohlberg			

9. Describe the purpose of each of the following developmental assessment tools:

Tool	Target Population	Purpose
Brazelton Neonatal Behavioral Assessment Scale		
Denver II		
Early Language Milestones Scale		
Life Experiences Survey		
Stress Audit		
Functional Activities Questionnaire		
Minimum Data Set for Nursing Facility Resident Assessment and Care Screening		
Folstein Mini-Mental State Examination		
Beck Depression Inventory		

Which tools can be self-administered or used by a caregiver?

_____

_____

_____

_____

_____

10. While you are performing a well-child exam on a 4-year-old, the mother tells you she is concerned about a lag in his motor and language skills. Which of the developmental assessment tools might be helpful?

_____

_____

_____

What gross motor skills and language skills should he be mastering?

_____

_____

_____

_____

11. Your patient, a 73-year-old widower, is being evaluated for symptoms of physical and mental decline. Which assessment tools might be helpful?

_____

_____

_____

What are the developmental tasks for your patient?

_____

_____

_____

_____

_____

Self-Assessment Quiz

1. The most frequently used theory of personality development is _____.

2. In which developmental stage would these life events most likely occur?

   _____ Getting married

   _____ Beginning menopause

   _____ Developing a conscience

   _____ Developing a basic sense of trust

   _____ Beginning self-care (feeding, dressing)

   _____ Adopting moral standards for behavior

   _____ Adjusting to rapid physical and sexual changes

3. True or false?

   ☐ **T** ☐ **F** A major task for a young adult is generativity.

   ☐ **T** ☐ **F** The Minimum Data Set (MDS) is required by law for nursing home residents.

   ☐ **T** ☐ **F** Egocentrism is a characterization of Piaget's sensorimotor stage.

   ☐ **T** ☐ **F** The Denver II is the most widely used developmental screening tool.

   ☐ **T** ☐ **F** Moral development (Kohlberg) parallels cognitive behavior development.

   ☐ **T** ☐ **F** Chronic diseases are often first diagnosed in early middle adulthood.

4. Match the following terms and descriptions.

   _____ Profiles personal-social, fine motor-adaptive, language, and gross motor skills

   _____ Predicts susceptibility to stress-related illness

   _____ Identifies at-risk adolescents

   _____ Assesses level of independence in performing ADLs

   _____ Can determine a need for further neurological examination

   _____ Tests comprehensibility, manageability, and meaningfulness

   A. Folstein MMSE

   B. Sense of Coherence Scale

   C. Functional Activities Questionnaire

   D. Denver II

   E. HEADSS

   F. Recent Life Changes Questionnaire

5. A _____ allows the elderly to evaluate their experiences, relationships, successes, and failures from the perspective of age.

Lab Practice for Cultural Assessment

Chapter 5

Learning Objectives

1. Compare characteristics of various cultures.
2. Identify components of a cultural assessment.
3. Conduct a comprehensive cultural assessment on your lab partner.
4. Identify cultural influences on health values and behaviors.

Reading Assignment

Before beginning this lab assignment, please read Chapter 5, Cultural Assessment, in *Health Assessment & Physical Examination* (3rd ed.) by Mary Ellen Zator Estes.

Key Terms

Please define the following terms:

acculturation _____

_____

bilingualism _____

_____

cross-cultural nursing care _____

_____

cultural beliefs _____

_____

cultural diversity _____

_____

cultural identity _____

_____

cultural norms _____

_____

cultural relativism _____

_____

cultural rituals _____

_____

cultural values _____

_____

culturally competent nursing care _____
_____

culture _____
_____

culture shock _____
_____

custom _____
_____

ecomap _____
_____

enculturation _____
_____

ethnic group _____
_____

ethnic identity _____
_____

ethnocentrism _____
_____

folk illness _____
_____

folk practitioner _____
_____

minority group members _____
_____

multicultural identity _____
_____

multiculturalism _____
_____

naturalistic illness _____
_____

personalistic illness _____
_____

race _____
_____

scientific illness _____
_____

subculture _____
_____

value orientation _____
_____

Laboratory Activities

1. Describe culturally competent nursing care.

   _____

   _____

   _____

   _____

   _____

   _____

   _____

2. Contrast racial and ethnic groups.

   _____

   _____

   _____

   _____

   Identify six ethnic groups usually recognized in the United States.

   A. _____

   B. _____

   C. _____

   D. _____

   E. _____

   F. _____

   Why is it useful to determine an individual's place of birth as well as his self-identified ethnic group?

   _____

   _____

   _____

3. Identify your own primary culture and the subcultures of which you are a member.

   _____

   _____

   _____

   _____

4. How does your lab partner view each of the following values?

   Time: What is your time orientation?

   _____

   Human Nature: What is the basic nature of human beings?

   _____

Activity: What is the primary purpose of life?

_____

Relational: What is the purpose of human relations?

_____

People to Nature: What is the relationship of human beings to nature?

_____

5. How might family and kinship patterns affect an individual's health care?

_____

_____

_____

6. What is the importance of self-care practices and home remedies to a patient?

_____

_____

_____

_____

7. Use the Echols-Armstrong Cultural Assessment tool in your text to interview your patient or lab partner.

Ethnic Group and Racial Background

How long have you lived here?　_____

Where were you born?　_____

Primary ethnic group?　_____

How closely do you identify with
this group?　_____

What has been your exposure to
health problems?　_____

Major Beliefs and Values

What traditions and beliefs are related
to your health practices?　_____

_____

Health Beliefs and Practices

What does it mean to be healthy
or sick?　_____

What do you do to stay healthy?　_____

What do you do when you are sick?　_____

Who makes health care decisions?　_____

Do you follow any cultural or ethnic
restrictions?　_____

Who do you prefer to provide
health care? _____

Language Barriers and Communication Styles
Which language do you prefer? _____
Do you need an interpreter for
health care? _____
What are your cultural preferences
for social contact? _____

Role of Family, Spousal Relationship, Parenting Styles
What is the ethnic background of
your family? _____
Who are members of your family? _____
Have there been any recent changes in
your health, work, or social patterns? _____
How can health care workers help you
achieve health and well-being? _____
_____

8. Contrast naturalistic illnesses and personalistic illnesses.

_____
_____
_____

Which cultures share the evil eye belief?

_____
_____

9. List one health value or custom that might have a positive influence and one that might have a
negative influence on medical treatment for each of the following cultural groups:

Cultural Group	Possible Positive Influence	Possible Negative Influence
Asian American		
Black American		
Hispanic American		
Native American		

Cultural Group	Possible Positive Influence	Possible Negative Influence
Middle Eastern American		
White American		

Self-Assessment Quiz

1. _____ is a learned and socially transmitted orientation and way of life of a group of people.

2. True or false?

   ☐ T ☐ F   The fastest-growing minority in the United States is Hispanic.

   ☐ T ☐ F   A diagram of an individual's relationships to family, friends, peers, and neighbors is called a *sociogram*.

   ☐ T ☐ F   Communication variables include eye contact, topic taboos, and who makes health care decisions in the family.

   ☐ T ☐ F   Asian, Middle Eastern, and Hispanic families are typically patriarchal.

   ☐ T ☐ F   Behaviors associated with healing, marriage, and worship are examples of values.

   ☐ T ☐ F   Cultural relativism is a belief that no culture is superior to another.

   ☐ T ☐ F   All cultural groups use self-care practices.

3. An informal process of adaptation to a dominant culture by new members from another culture is called _____.

4. Match the following cultural groups and characteristics.

   _____ Folk care practices include *cao gio* (rubbing skin with coin) and *bat gil* (skin pinching)

   _____ Health results from a balance between energy forces *yin* (cold) and *yang* (hot)

   _____ Use folk practices "first and last"

   _____ May use herbalists, midwives, or voodoo priests

   _____ Prevent and treat illness with "hot" and "cold" food prescriptions and prohibitions

   _____ Prayer is a common means for prevention and treatment of illness

   _____ May use a medicine man, diviner-diagnostician, and singers to help with illness

   _____ Emotional distress may be expressed as "heart disease"

   A. Haitian
   B. Native American
   C. Middle Eastern
   D. Black American
   E. Mexican
   F. Chinese
   G. Appalachian
   H. Vietnamese

5. Disorientation, uncertainty, and alienation that can occur during the process of adjusting are collectively called _____.

Lab Practice for Spiritual Assessment

Learning Objectives

1. Identify and compare characteristics of religious beliefs.
2. Conduct a spiritual assessment.
3. Identify signs that indicate a patient is experiencing spiritual distress.
4. Determine appropriate interactions with patients in spiritual distress.

Reading Assignment

Before beginning this lab assignment, please read Chapter 6, Spiritual Assessment, in *Health Assessment & Physical Examination* (3rd ed.) by Mary Ellen Zator Estes.

Key Terms

Please define the following terms:

advance directive _____

_____

agnostic _____

_____

animism _____

_____

atheist _____

_____

code of ethics _____

_____

cult _____

_____

dogma _____

_____

faith _____

_____

god _____

_____

heaven _____

_____

heretic _____

_____

holistic nursing _____

_____

monotheistic religion _____

_____

new age _____

_____

nirvana _____

_____

pagan _____

_____

pantheism _____

_____

parish nursing _____

_____

pastoral care _____

_____

polytheistic religion _____

_____

prayer _____

_____

reincarnation _____

_____

religion _____

_____

ritual _____

_____

schismatic _____

_____

sin_____

_____

soul _____

_____

spirit_____

_____

spiritual distress _____

_____

spirituality _____

_____

Laboratory Activities

1. Spiritual support may be helpful during times of change or crisis, such as:

   _____

   _____

   _____

   _____

   _____

2. Contrast spirituality and religion.

   _____

   _____

   _____

   _____

   _____

   _____

3. What information is included in the spiritual assessment?

   _____

   _____

   _____

   _____

   _____

   _____

   _____

4. What are signs that a patient may be experiencing spiritual distress?

   _____

   _____

   _____

   _____

   _____

5. Conduct a spiritual assessment on your patient or lab partner, beginning with the following questions and observations:

   A. Do you have an advance directive (living will or durable medical power of attorney)? _____

   _____

   B. Have you signed an organ donor card or thought about donating any organs or tissue after death?_____

   _____

   C. Do you have any spiritual or religious beliefs that may affect your health care? _____

   _____

   _____

D. Note any outward signs, such as religious clothing or jewelry, that may be related to the spiritual beliefs of the patient. _____
_____

E. Who should we notify if there is a change in your condition?_____
_____

F. Do you want me to notify a place of worship or a specific religious leader?_____
_____

G. What do you believe in?_____
_____
_____
_____
_____

H. What seems to help you when you are ill?_____
_____
_____
_____
_____

6. What nursing interventions are appropriate for the patient in spiritual distress?
_____
_____
_____
_____
_____
_____

7. What type of support can a hospital chaplain provide for the patient?
_____
_____
_____

8. Actions or statements you should avoid when intervening in the patient's spiritual condition include:
_____
_____
_____
_____
_____

Why are clichés inappropriate?

_____

_____

_____

9. What are signs that a patient may exhibit when spiritual distress has decreased?

_____

_____

_____

_____

Self-Assessment Quiz

1. What are two nursing diagnoses that address the spiritual care of the patient?

    A. _____

    B. _____

2. True or false?

    ☐ **T** ☐ **F**   The spiritual assessment is better if conducted as a stand-alone interview.

    ☐ **T** ☐ **F**   Spiritual beliefs help the patient define her ultimate purpose in life.

    ☐ **T** ☐ **F**   Hinduism is an example of a monotheistic religion.

    ☐ **T** ☐ **F**   Nursing interventions attempt to resolve spiritual distress.

    ☐ **T** ☐ **F**   Hospitals are required to conduct a spiritual history on all inpatients.

    ☐ **T** ☐ **F**   The question "What is your religion?" may be inappropriate.

3. Fill in the blanks:

    A. For some patients, _____ is an essential ingredient in health care.

    B. _____ is the belief that after death, the person lives another life on earth in another body.

    C. _____ refers to the essential beliefs at the core of a religion.

    D. _____ is the belief that all components of the universe have a life force.

    E. Birth, accidents, illness, and dying can provoke _____ in a patient.

4. The statement "It'll all look better tomorrow" is an example of a _____.

    The statement "It was God's will" is an example of a _____.

5. In which religion are these found? (Some may have more than one answer.)

   _____ Generally against donating or receiving organs

   _____ Life support is seen as unnatural and unnecessary

   _____ Holy water is poured into the mouth of a dying person

   _____ Birth control and infertility treatment are permitted

   _____ Good karma results from saving, prolonging, or improving life

   _____ Complex dietary rules may be observed by its members

   _____ Pork and pork products, alcohol, and street drugs are forbidden

   _____ Anointing of the sick with oil and prayers may be done often during an illness

   _____ Privacy should be maintained for females during hospitalization, with long-sleeved gowns if possible

   _____ After death, the body should not be disturbed with movement, talking, or crying

N Native American religions

B Buddhism

H Hinduism

I Islam

J Judaism

P Protestant

R Roman Catholic or Orthodox

Lab Practice for Nutritional Assessment

Learning Objectives

1. Describe the *Dietary Guidelines for Americans* 2005.
2. Complete a nutritional history and physical assessment.
3. Evaluate subjective and objective data to determine nutritional status.
4. Identify abnormal patterns of nutrition and diseases.

Reading Assignment

Before beginning this lab assignment, please read Chapter 7, Nutritional Assessment, in *Health Assessment & Physical Examination* (3rd ed.) by Mary Ellen Zator Estes.

Key Terms

Please define the following terms:

albumin _____

_____

anergy _____

_____

anthropometric measurements _____

_____

anticipatory guidance _____

_____

antigen skin testing _____

_____

atherosclerosis _____

_____

Body Mass Index _____

_____

cachexia_____

_____

carbohydrate_____

_____

cholesterol_____

_____

creatinine _____

_____

Dietary Reference Intakes _____

_____

fats _____

_____

fat-soluble vitamins _____

_____

hematocrit _____

_____

hemoglobin _____

_____

high-density lipoprotein _____

_____

hyperglycemia _____

_____

hypoglycemia _____

_____

kilocalorie _____

_____

kwashiorkor _____

_____

lactose intolerance _____

_____

low-density lipoprotein _____

_____

macromineral _____

_____

marasmus _____

_____

micromineral _____

_____

mid-arm circumference _____

_____

mid-arm muscle circumference _____

_____

mineral _____

_____

monosaturated fats _____

_____

nitrogen _____

_____

nutrient _____

_____

nutrition _____

_____

obesity _____

_____

omega-3 fatty acids _____

_____

osteoporosis _____

_____

pica _____

_____

prealbumin _____

_____

protein _____

_____

Recommended Dietary Allowance _____

_____

saturated fats _____

_____

serum iron _____

_____

skinfold thickness _____

_____

total iron-binding capacity _____

_____

transferrin _____

_____

triceps skinfold _____

_____

triglyceride _____

_____

vitamin _____

_____

water-soluble vitamin _____

_____

Laboratory Activities

1. List the nutritional sources of and functions for the following nutrients:

	Sources	Functions
Carbohydrates		
Proteins		
Fats		
Vitamin A		
Niacin		
Folacin		
Potassium		
Magnesium		

2. Each age group has special physical and psychological characteristics that can affect nutritional status. What are some of these characteristics, and what suggestions could you offer to maintain a healthy nutritional status?

	Characteristics	Suggestions
Infants		
Toddlers		
Preschoolers		
School-age children		
Adolescents		

Characteristics	Suggestions
Young and middle-aged adults	
Pregnant or lactating women	
Older adults	

3. What are the signs and symptoms of dehydration?

_____

_____

_____

_____

_____

4. You will now complete a nutritional assessment, including a nutritional history, physical assessment, and anthropometric measurements. Perform the nutritional history by asking your patient or lab partner the questions in Part 1 and completing the food intake history in Part 2.

PART 1: Diet History

Do you follow a particular diet?

_____

What are your food likes and dislikes? Do you have any cravings?

_____

How do you prepare and store food?

_____

Do you eat alone or with others?

_____

Has there been any change in your weight?

_____

Has there been any change in your appetite or dietary habits?

_____

Have you had any difficulty with feeding yourself, eating, chewing, or swallowing?

_____

Do you take vitamins, supplements, or liquid diets?

_____

Have you had any fatigue, weakness, or frequent infections?

_____

Has there been a change in your skin, nails, or hair?

_____

Do you have any mouth sores?

_____

Do you have any vision changes or eye discharge?

_____

Do you have any headaches, irritability, or numbness?

_____

Has there been any change in your appetite or any nausea, diarrhea, or constipation?

_____

Do you have pain, cramping, or frequent fractures?

_____

(Female) Has there been any change in your menstrual pattern?

_____

PART 2: Food Intake History (24-Hour Diet Recall)

_____

_____

_____

_____

_____

5. **Physical Assessment.** (*Equipment: Scale with right-angle headboard, tape measure, skinfold calipers.*) Refer to Table 7-10 in your text and note any objective signs of poor nutritional status to complete the following information:

General appearance _____

Skin, hair, nails _____

Eyes _____

Mouth _____

Head and neck _____

Heart and peripheral vasculature   _____

Abdomen   _____

Musculoskeletal system   _____

Neurological system   _____

Anthropometric Measurements

Determine the anthropometric measurements for your lab partner.

Height: _____

Weight: _____

% ideal body weight $= \dfrac{\text{current weight}}{\text{IBW}} \times 100 =$ _____

% usual body weight $= \dfrac{\text{current weight}}{\text{usual body weight}} \times 100 =$ _____

% weight change $= \dfrac{\text{usual weight} - \text{current weight}}{\text{usual weight}} \times 100 =$ _____

Body Mass Index (BMI) $= \dfrac{\text{weight (in kg)}}{\text{m}^2} =$ _____   Is BMI within normal limits? _____
$\qquad$ (m = height in meters)

Waist/hip ratio $= \dfrac{\text{waist (in inches)}}{\text{hip (in inches)}} =$ _____   Is waist/hip ratio normal? _____

Triceps skinfold (TSF) = _____ mm   Convert to cm = _____ cm

Mid-arm circumference (MAC) = _____ cm

Mid-arm muscle circumference (MAMC)

$\quad$ MAMC (cm) = MAC (cm) $-$ [3.14 $\times$ TSF (in cm)] = _____   Is MAMC normal? _____

Laboratory Data (optional)

Hematocrit/hemoglobin   _____

Cholesterol and triglycerides   _____

Transferrin, total iron-binding
   capacity, and iron   _____

Total lymphocyte count   _____

Antigen skin testing   _____

Albumin   _____

Glucose   _____

Creatinine height index   _____

Nitrogen balance   _____

6. What is your assessment of your patient's or lab partner's nutritional status? Do you have any recommendations?

   _____

   _____

   _____

   _____

7. An 18-year-old female's TSF is 8 mm. Her MAC is 230 mm. Calculate her MAMC.

   _____

   _____

   _____

   _____

   What nutritional recommendations could you offer?

   _____

   _____

   _____

8. What questions would you include in a diet history for the patient who is pregnant?

   _____

   _____

   _____

   _____

   _____

9. List five signs and symptoms of poor nutritional status that are noted in the skin and mouth.

   A. _____

   B. _____

   C. _____

   D. _____

   E. _____

10. The five risk factors associated with metabolic syndrome include:

   A. _____

   B. _____

   C. _____

   D. _____

   E. _____

11. What nutritional difficulties often arise in the aging population?

_____
_____
_____
_____
_____

How can you individualize nutritional recommendations to meet the special needs of the aging population?

_____
_____
_____

Self-Assessment Quiz

1. As part of a complete nutritional assessment, anticipatory guidance includes:

_____
_____
_____
_____

2. Match these diseases with their findings:

_____ Deficiency of vitamin C	A. kwashiorkor
_____ Reduced bone mass	B. marasmus
_____ Softening and deformities of the bones	C. anorexia nervosa
_____ Affects primarily infants	D. bulimia nervosa
_____ Occurs most often in children ages 1 to 4	E. osteoporosis
_____ Shows compensatory behavior to avoid weight gain	F. pica
_____ Involves non-food cravings	G. scurvy
_____ Includes amenorrhea	H. rickets
_____ Deficiency of vitamin D	
_____ Body weight less than 85% of expected weight	
_____ Risk factors include family hx and estrogen deficiency	

3. List the eight subject areas outlined in the Dietary Guidelines for Americans 2005.

A. _____   E. _____
B. _____   F. _____
C. _____   G. _____
D. _____   H. _____

4. Which of the following patients might cause you the most concern, and why?

Patient A: A 3-year-old seems to be eating less than his younger brother. He enjoys fruit juices and milk but has shown a decline in his previously rapid growth rate. He often refuses to eat more than just one food at a meal.

Patient B: A 17-year-old female spends much of her time looking in the mirror and feels she probably does not look as good as her classmates. She has become more physically active and occasionally skips meals.

Patient C: A new mother who is breastfeeding her baby happily reports her loss of several pounds of "baby fat" since the birth one month ago. She reports eating a "good diet," with 8 ounces of juice or water four times a day.

Patient D: A 75-year-old patient who lives alone, but has family nearby, has been eating a little less and occasionally feels constipated. Her dentures do not fit well anymore. She tells her family that she does not eat as much because "I can't taste it, anyway."

_____

_____

_____

_____

_____

5. Fill in the blanks:

   A. Water is essential to life and accounts for _____% of the body's weight.

   B. *Obesity* is defined as a weight greater than _____% of the ideal body weight.

   C. Protein should account for _____% of the diet for an adult.

   D. More than _____% of patients with anorexia nervosa are female.

6. A patient diagnosed with metabolic syndrome is at increased risk for _____ and _____.

Lab Practice for Physical Assessment Techniques

Chapter 8

Learning Objectives

1. Practice physical assessment techniques.
2. Identify and describe characteristics of percussion sounds.
3. Establish a systematic order for assessment procedures.
4. Demonstrate patient positioning and draping techniques.

Reading Assignment

Before beginning this lab assignment, please read Chapter 8, Physical Assessment Techniques, in *Health Assessment & Physical Examination* (3rd ed.) by Mary Ellen Zator Estes.

Key Terms

Please define the following terms:

auscultation _____

_____

deep palpation _____

_____

direct auscultation _____

_____

direct fist percussion _____

_____

direct percussion _____

_____

dullness _____

_____

duration (of percussion) _____

_____

flatness _____

_____

hyperresonance _____

_____

immediate auscultation _____

_____

immediate percussion _____

indirect auscultation _____

indirect fist percussion _____

indirect percussion _____

inspection _____

intensity (of percussion) _____

light palpation _____

mediate auscultation _____

mediate percussion _____

palpation _____

percussion _____

pitch (of percussion) _____

pleximeter _____

plexor _____

quality (of percussion) _____

resonance _____

standard precautions _____

tangential lighting _____

transmission-based precautions _____

tympany _____

Laboratory Activities

1. Which part of your hand is most useful in assessing each of the following?

   Temperature _____

   Vibration _____

   Masses _____

   Edema _____

   Pulsations _____

   Fine tactile discrimination _____

2. Assist your lab partner into each of the following positions for patient examination (refer to Figure 8-13 in your text). Use a drape as appropriate.

semi-Fowler's	side lying
sitting (high Fowler's)	lithotomy
horizontal recumbent	knee-chest
dorsal recumbent	Sims'

3. In what order do you usually perform these physical assessment techniques?

   _____ Palpation

   _____ Auscultation

   _____ Inspection

   _____ Percussion

   How and why does this pattern change for assessing the abdomen?

   _____

   _____

   _____

   _____

4. Practice the technique of indirect percussion on your lab partner to elicit different sounds. What sounds are produced over each of the following?

   Gastric bubble_____

   Lungs _____

   Muscle/bones _____

   Liver (organs) _____

5. Complete the following chart on the characteristics of percussion sounds:

	Location	Intensity	Duration	Pitch	Quality
Tympany					
Hyperresonance					
Resonance					
Dullness					
Flatness					

6. Percuss the frontal and maxillary sinuses with immediate or direct percussion and the kidneys with mediate or indirect fist percussion. Do you note any tenderness?

7. What is the difference between light and deep palpation?

8. Describe the correct use of the stethoscope for indirect (mediate) auscultation.

9. Identify strategies to promote a trusting and caring relationship with your patient.

Self-Assessment Quiz

1. Name the four types of percussion.

   A. _____

   B. _____

   C. _____

   D. _____

   Which is the preferred method for kidney assessment?

   _____

2. True or false?

   ☐ **T** ☐ **F**   Use the diaphragm of the stethoscope to listen for bruits and murmurs.

   ☐ **T** ☐ **F**   Hold the bell firmly on the skin surface to be auscultated.

   ☐ **T** ☐ **F**   Always conduct an assessment in a systematic fashion.

   ☐ **T** ☐ **F**   Frequency (or pitch) is caused by a sound's vibrations.

   ☐ **T** ☐ **F**   Earpieces on the stethoscope should point slightly away from the nose.

   ☐ **T** ☐ **F**   The bell transmits low-pitched sounds.

   ☐ **T** ☐ **F**   The most important aspect of infection control is the consistent and proper use of gloves.

3. Name each of the following positions:

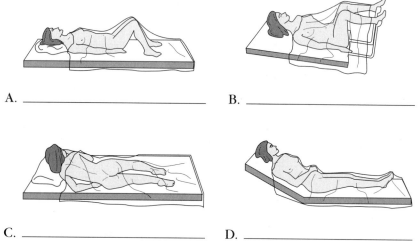

   A. _____   B. _____

   C. _____   D. _____

4. Match the following sounds:

_____ Predominant sound over the abdomen

_____ May indicate emphysema

_____ Heard over bone or muscle

_____ Has a "hollow" quality

_____ Noted over the liver

_____ The sound with the shortest duration

_____ Predominant sound over the lungs

A. flat

B. dull

C. resonant

D. hyperresonant

E. tympany

5. What are the four main purposes of a physical assessment?

A. _____

B. _____

C. _____

D. _____

Lab Practice for General Survey, Vital Signs, and Pain

Chapter
9

Learning Objectives

1. Demonstrate a general survey, including physical and psychological presence and any distress.
2. Assess vital signs and pain using appropriate techniques.
3. Locate anatomical sites for pulse assessment.
4. Describe factors affecting vital signs.
5. Identify normal and abnormal findings.

Reading Assignment

Before beginning this lab assignment, please read Chapter 9, General Survey, Vital Signs, and Pain, in *Health Assessment & Physical Examination* (3rd ed.) by Mary Ellen Zator Estes.

Key Terms

Please define the following terms:

aneroid manometer _____

_____

apnea _____

_____

arrhythmia _____

_____

asystole _____

_____

auscultatory gap _____

_____

baroreceptors _____

_____

blood pressure _____

_____

bradycardia _____

_____

bradypnea _____

_____

circadian rhythm _____

_____

diastole _____

_____

dysrhythmia_____

_____

hypertension_____

_____

hyperthermia _____

_____

hypotension _____

_____

hypothermia _____

_____

Korotkoff sounds _____

_____

mercury manometer _____

_____

nociception_____

_____

nociceptors_____

_____

pain _____

_____

peripheral vasculature resistance _____

_____

pulse _____

_____

pulse deficit_____

_____

pulse pressure_____

_____

respiration_____

_____

sphygmomanometer _____

_____

systole _____

_____

tachycardia _____

_____

tachypnea _____

_____

temperature _____

_____

vital signs_____

_____

Laboratory Activities

1. List several indicators of distress in a patient.

    _____

    _____

    _____

2. Complete this 4-point scale for measuring pulse volume.

    _____

    +0
    _____

    +1
    _____

    +2
    _____

    +3
    _____

    +4
    _____

3. Try to palpate the following pulses on your patient or lab partner. Use a Doppler if needed.

temporal	brachial	popliteal
carotid	radial	posterior tibial
apical	femoral	dorsalis pedis

    Using the stick figure below, document your findings.

4. How do you convert degrees of temperature:

From Celsius to Fahrenheit? _____

From Fahrenheit to Celsius? _____

5. Name one advantage and one disadvantage of each of these four basic routes for measuring body temperature.

	Advantage	Disadvantage
Oral		
Rectal		
Axillary		
Tympanic		

6. Blood pressure cuffs come in several sizes. How do you determine the correct size for your patient?

_____

_____

_____

_____

_____

7. **Physical Exam.** *(Equipment: Stethoscope, watch with a second hand, thermometer, sphygmo-manometer.)* Follow the physical assessment guidelines in your text to complete the following information.

General Survey

Physical presence

Stated age versus apparent age   looks age 33 yrs old

General appearance   looks healthy

Body fat   5'4", 199 lbs

Stature   Slouched posture

Motor activity   not active, smooth, effortless

Body and breath odors   clean, no aparent odour

Psychological presence

Dress, grooming, and personal
hygiene   Clean, neatly dressed, appropriate for weather

Mood and manner   *pleasent, friendly*
Speech   *Clear and understandable*
Facial expression   *alert, smiling*
Distress   *Coughing when moving a lot*

Vital Signs
Respiration   *22 breaths per min*
Pulse   *84 beats per min*
Temperature   _____
Blood pressure (document   *126/72*
   as shown in Nursing Tip.)

Pain (indicate which pain
   assessment tool used.)   *Denies*
Patient's description of pain _____
_____
_____
_____
_____

8. Name three conditions that can cause a patient to have strong body or breath odors.
   A. _____
   B. _____
   C. _____

What can cause each of the following errors in blood pressure measurement?

Inaccurately high BP _____
High diastolic BP_____
Inaccurately low BP _____
Low systolic BP_____

9. Write out this formula for arterial blood pressure:

$$MAP = CO \times TPR$$

_____
_____

10. Your adult patient has a screening blood pressure reading of 166/112. What is your recommendation for follow-up?

_____
_____
_____
_____

11. What are the variables that affect pain?

_____

_____

Responses to pain may include

_____

_____

_____

_____

_____

Self-Assessment Quiz

1. Under which of the following assessments would each patient observation be noted?

_____ Flat affect	A. stated or apparent age
_____ Tremors and tics	B. body fat
_____ Diaphoresis	C. stature
_____ Thin, frail	D. motor activity
_____ Ataxia	E. body/breath odor
_____ Slumped	F. personal hygiene
_____ Long limbs	G. mood and manner
_____ Disheveled	H. speech
_____ Slurring	I. facial expression
_____ Wheezing	J. distress
_____ Aphasia	

2. Label the pulse sites in the following diagram.

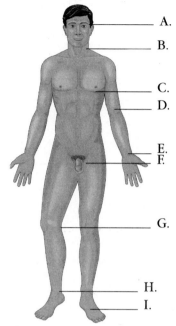

    A.

    B.

    C.

    D.

    E.

    F.

    G.

    H.

    I.

3. List four factors that can affect blood pressure.

    A. _____

    B. _____

    C. _____

    D. _____

4. True or false?

    ☐ **T** ☐ **F** Oxygen therapy can affect a patient's oral temperature reading.

    ☐ **T** ☐ **F** The lower edge of the blood pressure cuff should just cover the antecubital fossa.

    ☐ **T** ☐ **F** Hypothermia is a body temperature below 35°C.

    ☐ **T** ☐ **F** Phase III of the Korotkoff sounds is heard as clear, intense tapping.

    ☐ **T** ☐ **F** The resting pulse rate of a 14-year-old is about the same as that of an adult.

    ☐ **T** ☐ **F** Bradycardia in an adult is a pulse rate below 60; tachycardia is above 110.

    ☐ **T** ☐ **F** A difference of greater than 5 to 10 mm Hg between the blood pressures of the right and the left arms is abnormal.

5. Convert the following body temperatures:

    A. 37°C = _____°F   C. 97.6°F = _____°C

    B. 38°C = _____°F   D. 101°F = _____°C

6. Identify two pain intensity scales that would be helpful to use with a school-age child.

    _____

    _____

Lab Practice for Skin, Hair, and Nails

Chapter
10

Learning Objectives

1. Conduct a review of systems (ROS) for the skin, hair, and nails.
2. Demonstrate a physical assessment of the integumentary system.
3. Describe the characteristics of primary and secondary skin lesions.
4. List the danger signs for cancerous lesions.

Reading Assignment

Before beginning this lab assignment, please read Chapter 10, Skin, Hair, and Nails, in *Health Assessment & Physical Examination* (3rd ed.) by Mary Ellen Zator Estes.

Key Terms

Please define the following terms:

albinism _____

_____

alopecia _____

_____

anemia _____

_____

apocrine glands _____

_____

arrector pili muscle _____

_____

carotenemia _____

_____

cherry angioma _____

_____

cyanosis _____

_____

dehydration _____

_____

dermis _____

_____

desquamation _____

ecchymosis _____

eccrine glands _____

edema _____

eleidin _____

epidermis _____

granulation tissue _____

hirsutism _____

hyperthermia _____

hypothermia _____

integumentary system _____

jaundice _____

keratosis _____

lentigo _____

lesion _____

lichenification _____

lunula _____

mast cells _____

matrix _____

melanocytes _____

nailbed _____

_____

nail plate _____

_____

nail root _____

_____

nevi _____

_____

papillary layer _____

_____

periungual tissue _____

_____

petechiae _____

_____

polycythemia _____

_____

pruritus _____

_____

purpura _____

_____

rash _____

_____

reepithelialization _____

_____

reticular layer _____

_____

sebaceous glands _____

_____

seborrhea _____

_____

sebum _____

_____

spider angioma _____

_____

stratum corneum _____

_____

stratum germinativum _____

_____

stratum granulosum _____

_____

stratum lucidum _____

_____

stratum spinosum _____

_____

subcutaneous tissue _____

_____

sweat glands _____

_____

terminal hair _____

_____

turgor _____

_____

vellus hair _____

_____

venous star _____

_____

vitiligo _____

_____

xerosis _____

_____

Laboratory Activities

1. Label the following items on the drawing:

    artery
    dermis
    epidermis
    hair follicle
    nerve
    sebaceous (oil) gland
    sensory nerve ending
    subcutaneous tissue
    sweat gland (eccrine)
    sweat pore
    vein

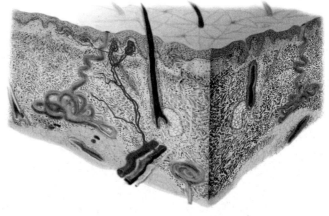

2. How do apocrine and eccrine glands differ?

    _____

    _____

    _____

    _____

3. List five main functions of the skin.

    A. _____

    B. _____

    C. _____

    D. _____

    E. _____

4. What normal variations in color may be noted on a dark-skinned patient?

    _____

    _____

    _____

5. What is the difference between a primary and a secondary lesion?

    _____

    _____

    _____

6. If a lesion is present, what characteristics will you describe?

    _____

    _____

    _____

7. If your patient presented with a skin rash, what questions would you ask for the HPI?

    _____

    _____

    _____

    _____

    _____

8. **ROS (Review of Systems).** Ask your lab partner the following questions:

    Do you have any history of skin disease?

    _____

    Do you have unusually dry or moist skin?

    _____

    Do you have any burning, itching, or bruising?

    _____

    *Do you have any food, drug, or environmental
    allergies?*

    _____

Do you have any skin rashes or lesions?

_____

Do you have any changes in skin color,
pigmentation, or moles?

_____

Do you have any changes in or loss of hair?

_____

How do you care for your skin, hair,
and nails? (Refer to Nursing Checklist in your text.)

_____

9. **Physical Exam.** *(Equipment: Light source, small centimeter ruler, magnifying glass, gloves.)*
    Follow the physical assessment guidelines in your text to complete the following information.

    Inspection of the Skin
    Color   _____
    Bleeding, ecchymosis, vascularity   _____
    Lesions   _____
                                                            _____
                                                            _____
                                                            _____

    Palpation of the Skin
    Moisture   _____
    Temperature   _____
    Tenderness   _____
    Texture   _____
    Turgor   _____
    Edema

    Inspection of the Hair
    Color   _____
    Distribution   _____
    Lesions   _____

    Palpation of the Hair
    Texture   _____

    Inspection of the Nails
    Color   _____
    Shape and configuration   _____

Palpation of the Nails

Texture _____

10. What are the danger signs for potentially cancerous lesions?

   _____
   _____
   _____
   _____
   _____

11. How do you determine if edema is present?

   _____
   _____
   _____

   Complete this 4-point grading scale for edema.

   _____
   +0
   _____
   +1
   _____
   +2
   _____
   +3
   _____
   +4
   _____

12. How does cyanosis appear in light-skinned and dark-skinned patients?

   _____
   _____
   _____

   Explain why cyanosis may not be an accurate predictor of oxygen status.

   _____
   _____
   _____
   _____

13. What assessment findings might be signs of abuse?

   _____
   _____
   _____

14. How would you expect the skin, hair, and nails of a 72-year-old patient to differ from those of a younger patient?

Skin: _____

_____

_____

Hair: _____

_____

_____

Nails: _____

_____

_____

What advice could you give to your elderly patients to help them avoid skin damage?

_____

_____

_____

_____

_____

Self-Assessment Quiz

1. What are some of the characteristics of the skin that you would note on an examination?

_____

_____

_____

_____

_____

2. Which of the following shows an abnormal nail angle?

A.   B.   C.

3. Identify each of these skin lesions as primary (P) or secondary (S).

_____ Tumor	_____ Papule	_____ Cyst
_____ Keloid	_____ Fissure	_____ Lichenification
_____ Erosion	_____ Ulcer	_____ Pustule
_____ Vesicle	_____ Crust	_____ Scar

4. Match the definition with the correct term.

_____ Localized edema in the epidermis with irregular elevation	A. vesicle
_____ Fibrous tissue that replaces dermal tissue after injury	B. tumor
_____ Solid and elevated, deeper than a papule, over 2 cm	C. freckle
_____ Vesicles or bullae filled with pus, less than 0.5 cm diameter	D. scar
_____ Elevated mass containing serous fluid, less than 0.5 cm	E. excoriation
_____ Localized change in skin color, less than 1 cm diameter	F. wheal
_____ Loss of epidermal layers, exposing the dermis	G. cyst
_____ Encapsulated fluid-filled or semi-solid mass in subcutaneous tissue or dermis	H. pustule

5. Match each lesion with the appropriate diagram.

linear
zosteriform
annular
confluent

A._____ B._____ C._____ D._____

6. What does each letter represent in the ABCDE mnemonic for evaluating skin lesions?

A. _____   D. _____

B. _____   E. _____

C. _____

Lab Practice for Head, Neck, and Regional Lymphatics

Chapter 11

Learning Objectives

1. Conduct a review of systems (ROS) for the head and neck.
2. Locate anatomical structures of the head and neck.
3. Demonstrate appropriate physical assessment techniques.
4. Differentiate normal and abnormal findings.

Reading Assignment

Before beginning this lab assignment, please read Chapter 11, Head, Neck, and Regional Lymphatics, in *Health Assessment & Physical Examination* (3rd ed.) by Mary Ellen Zator Estes.

Key Terms

Please define the following terms:

acromegaly _____

_____

anterior triangle _____

_____

atlas _____

_____

axis _____

_____

Bell's palsy _____

_____

bregma _____

_____

craniotabes _____

_____

Down syndrome _____

_____

goiter _____

_____

hydrocephalus _____

_____

hypertelorism _____
_____

isthmus (of the thyroid) _____
_____

lipoma _____
_____

posterior triangle _____
_____

sutures _____
_____

torticollis _____
_____

vertebra prominens _____
_____

Laboratory Activities

1. Label the following nodes on the drawing:

   occipital
   posterior auricular
   posterior cervical
   preauricular
   submandibular
   submental
   superficial and deep cervical
   supraclavicular
   tonsillar

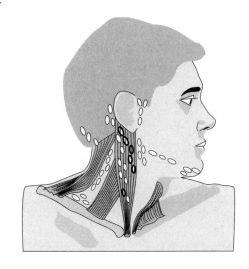

2. Locate each of the following on your lab partner:

   sternocleidomastoid muscle   mastoid process
   trapezius muscle   mandible
   temporomandibular joint   thyroid
   clavicle   trachea
   thyroid cartilage   external jugular vein
   cricoid cartilage   vertebra prominens

3. Locate the anterior and posterior cervical triangles on your lab partner. What anatomical features outline each of these areas?

   Anterior: _____

   _____

   Posterior: _____

   _____

4. On your lab partner, practice palpating the lymph nodes in a systematic order:

   preauricular
   postauricular
   occipital
   submental
   submandibular
   tonsillar
   anterior cervical chain
   posterior cervical chain
   supraclavicular

5. **ROS (Review of Systems).** Ask your patient or lab partner the following questions:

   Do you have any history of thyroid, sinus, or related illness?

   _____

   Have you had any surgery on the head or neck?

   _____

   Do you have any history of head injury?

   _____

   Do you have severe or frequent headaches?

   _____

   Do you have any neck pain, tenderness, or swelling?

   _____

   Do you have severe or frequent sore throats?

   _____

   Have you had any change in voice, any hoarseness, or any difficulty swallowing?

   _____

   Have there been any changes in your sleep patterns or weight?

   _____

6. **Physical Exam.** *(Equipment: Stethoscope, cup of water, penlight.)* Follow the physical assessment guidelines in your text to complete the following information.

Inspection of Shape of the Head _____

Palpation of the Head _____

**Inspection and Palpation
of the Scalp** _____

Inspection of the Face
Symmetry _____
Shape and features _____

**Palpation and Auscultation
of the Mandible** _____

**Inspection and Palpation
of the Neck**
Inspection of the neck _____
Palpation of the neck _____

Inspection of the Thyroid Gland _____

Palpation of the Thyroid Gland
Anterior or posterior approach _____

Auscultation of the Thyroid Gland _____

**Inspection and Palpation
of the Lymph Nodes** _____
_____

7. Examination of the cranial nerves is integrated into a head and neck assessment. How do you evaluate these cranial nerves?

CN No.	Name	Method of Evaluation
V		
VII		
XI		

8. What is the technique for assessing the trachea and carotid arteries?

   _____

   _____

   _____

9. Which findings from the history and physical exam might indicate thyroid cancer?

   _____

   _____

   _____

10. List four variations that you might see on the head and neck of an elderly patient.
    A. _____
    B. _____
    C. _____
    D. _____

Self-Assessment Quiz

1. Draw an outline around the anterior and posterior cervical triangles on this diagram.

   List the anatomical features that are located within the:

   A. anterior triangle

      _____

      _____

      _____

   B. posterior triangle

      _____

      _____

      _____

2. Match the following:

   _____ Facial asymmetry caused by cranial nerve damage   A. craniosynostosis

   _____ Caused by premature closure of sutures of the skull   B. myxedema

   _____ Abnormal enlargement of the skull and face
                                                                    C. Bell's palsy
   _____ Associated with hypothyroidism

   _____ Autoimmune disorder with increased levels of T_3 and T_4 D. crepitus

   _____ Sometimes noted in an exam of the TMJ   E. acromegaly

                                                                    F. Graves' disease

3. Label the anatomy in this diagram.

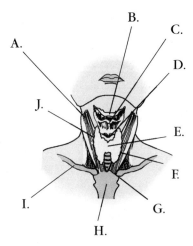

4. Identify at least four risk factors for migraine headache.

A. _____   C. _____

B. _____   D. _____

5. Label each of these findings normal or abnormal.

_____ No visible movement of the thyroid while swallowing

_____ Slight lateral deviation of the neck

_____ Small, discrete, movable nodes found on palpation

_____ Solitary nodule in the thyroid tissue

_____ Rubbery, nontender cervical nodes

Lab Practice for Eyes

Chapter
12

Learning Objectives

1. Locate anatomical structures of the eyes.
2. Conduct a review of systems (ROS) for the eyes.
3. Gain competency in using the ophthalmoscope.
4. Demonstrate a physical assessment of the eyes.

Reading Assignment

Before beginning this lab assignment, please read Chapter 12, Eyes, in *Health Assessment & Physical Examination* (3rd ed.) by Mary Ellen Zator Estes.

Key Terms

Please define the following terms:

accommodation _____

_____

amblyopia _____

_____

anisocoria _____

_____

anterior chamber _____

_____

arcus senilis _____

_____

blepharitis _____

_____

bulbar conjunctiva _____

_____

canthus _____

_____

caruncle _____

_____

cataract _____

_____

chalazion _____

_____

chemosis _____

_____

choroid _____

_____

ciliary body _____

_____

coloboma_____

_____

cone _____

_____

cornea _____

_____

dacryoadenitis_____

_____

dacryocystitis _____

_____

ectropion _____

_____

entropion _____

_____

esophoria_____

_____

esotropia _____

_____

exophoria _____

_____

exophthalmos _____

_____

exotropia_____

_____

fovea centralis_____

_____

glaucoma_____

_____

hordeolum_____

_____

hyperopia _____

_____

hyphema _____

injection _____

iris _____

lacrimal apparatus _____

lagophthalmos _____

lens _____

limbus _____

macula _____

myopia _____

nystagmus _____

optic disc _____

palpebral conjunctiva _____

palpebral fissure _____

phoria _____

physiologic cup _____

pinguecula _____

posterior chamber _____

presbyopia _____

pterygium _____

ptosis _____

puncta _____

_____

pupil _____

_____

retina _____

_____

rod _____

_____

sclera _____

_____

Snellen chart _____

_____

strabismus _____

_____

tarsal plates _____

_____

vitreous humor _____

_____

xanthelasma _____

_____

Laboratory Activities

1. Label the following diagram of the eye.

   anterior chamber
   cornea
   iris
   lens
   macula
   optic disc
   optic nerve
   pupil
   retina
   sclera
   veins and arteries

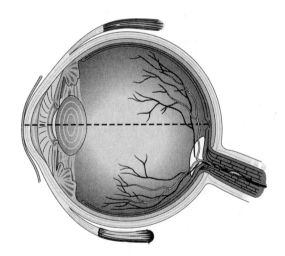

2. How and when would you use the negative and positive diopter settings on the ophthalmoscope?

   _____

   _____

   _____

   _____

   _____

3. What anatomical features are you assessing in the retina?

   _____

   _____

   _____

   _____

   _____

4. How do you test the corneal light reflex?

   _____

   _____

   _____

   If your patient has an abnormal finding, what additional testing will you do?

   _____

   _____

5. What does the confrontation test assess? Which cranial nerve is tested?

   _____

   _____

   _____

   _____

6. What do the cardinal fields of gaze assess?

   _____

   _____

   How do you perform this test?

   _____

   _____

   _____

Write in the name and number of the cranial nerve that controls each of the eye movements indicated in the following figure.

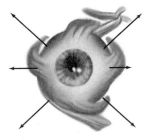 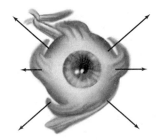

Right eye   **Left eye**

7. How would you assess the direct and consensual light reflexes?

_____

_____

_____

_____

8. **ROS (Review of Systems).** Ask your patient or lab partner the following questions:

Have you had any injury or surgery to the eyes?

_____

Do you have any hx of crossed eyes?

_____

Have you had any change in or loss of vision?

_____

Do you have any eye pain or frequent headaches?

_____

Do you have excessive tearing or dryness?

_____

Do you use glasses or contact lenses?

_____

When was your last vision exam/glaucoma testing?

_____

Do you use eye drops (Rx or OTC)?

_____

9. **Physical Exam.** *(Equipment: Snellen chart, Rosenbaum near-vision pocket screening card, ophthalmoscope, penlight, cotton-tipped applicator, gloves.)* Follow the physical assessment guidelines in your text to complete the following information.

Visual acuity

    Distance vision   _____

    Near vision   _____

    Color vision   _____

Visual fields   _____

External eye and lacrimal apparatus

    Eyelids   _____

    Lacrimal apparatus   _____

        Inspection   _____

        Palpation   _____

Extraocular muscle function

    Corneal light reflex   _____

    Cover/uncover test   _____

    Cardinal fields of gaze   _____

Anterior segment structures

    Conjunctiva   _____

    Sclera   _____

    Cornea   _____

    Anterior chamber   _____

    Iris   _____

    Pupil   _____

    Lens   _____

Posterior segment structures

    Retinal structures   _____

     _____

    Macula   _____

10. What abnormal findings might be noted during the eye examination on a patient with diabetes mellitus?

_____

_____

_____

Identify abnormal findings that may occur in a patient with hypertension.

_____

_____

_____

11. How would you determine if your patient has glaucoma?

    _____

    _____

    _____

12. You are performing an eye examination on your 72-year-old male patient. List several significant changes in his eyes and vision that you would anticipate.

    _____

    _____

    _____

    What are the three most common visual problems in the elderly population?

    A. _____

    B. _____

    C. _____

Self-Assessment Quiz

1. The area of central vision in the macula is called the _____.

2. Label the diagram of the retina.

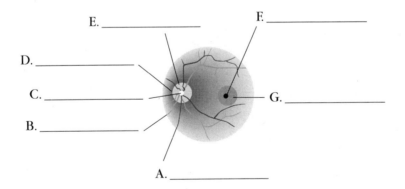

E. _____   F. _____

D. _____

C. _____   G. _____

B. _____

A. _____

    Is this a diagram of the right eye or the left eye? _____

3. Match these terms with the correct description:

_____ Area with a pinpoint reflective center

_____ Tests CN III, IV, and VI

_____ Dilated pupils

_____ Can be normal in lateral gaze

_____ Constricted pupils

_____ Tests for peripheral vision

_____ Causes disconjugate vision

_____ Loss of accommodation for near vision

_____ Abnormal finding in the retina

A. strabismus

B. presbyopia

C. confrontation

D. neovascularization

E. macula

F. cardinal fields of gaze

G. nystagmus

H. mydriasis

I. miosis

4. True or false?

☐ **T** ☐ **F**   The ratio of the cup diameter to the disc is 1:2.

☐ **T** ☐ **F**   Accommodation occurs when pupils constrict in response to light.

☐ **T** ☐ **F**   The inferior rectus muscle allows the eye to move down and out.

☐ **T** ☐ **F**   Progressively blurred distance vision is a symptom of a senile cataract.

☐ **T** ☐ **F**   Retinal veins are larger and darker than arteries and have a light reflex.

☐ **T** ☐ **F**   EOMs assess for visual fields.

5. The medical term for:

A. a "sty" is _____.

B. "nearsightedness" is _____.

6. What is a common definition of "legal" blindness?

_____

_____

Lab Practice for Ears, Nose, Mouth, and Throat

Learning Objectives

1. Locate anatomical structures of the ears, nose, mouth, and throat.
2. Conduct a review of systems (ROS) for the ears, nose, mouth, and throat.
3. Gain competency in using the otoscope.
4. Demonstrate appropriate physical assessment techniques.

Reading Assignment

Before beginning this lab assignment, please read Chapter 13, Ears, Nose, Mouth, and Throat, in *Health Assessment & Physical Examination* (3rd ed.) by Mary Ellen Zator Estes.

Key Terms

Please define the following terms:

auricle _____

_____

cerumen _____

_____

cochlea _____

_____

conchae _____

_____

eustachian tube _____

_____

frenulum (of the mouth) _____

_____

labyrinth _____

_____

linear raphe _____

_____

ossicles _____

_____

otitis media _____

_____

papilla _____

_____

paranasal sinuses _____

_____

pinna _____

_____

presbycusis _____

_____

Rinne test _____

_____

semicircular canals _____

_____

Stensen's ducts _____

_____

sulcus terminalis _____

_____

turbinates _____

_____

uvula _____

_____

vestibule (of the ear) _____

_____

Weber test _____

_____

Wharton's ducts _____

_____

Laboratory Activities

1. Label the following diagram of a cross-section of the ear.

CN VIII
cochlea
eustachian tube
external auditory canal
helix
incus
malleus
round window
semicircular canals
stapes
tympanic membrane

Draw a circle around the middle ear.

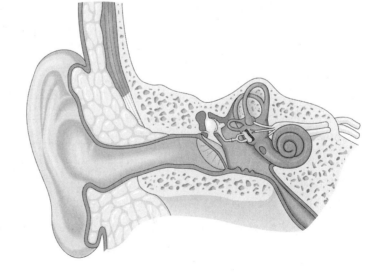

2. What are the two pathways for hearing?

   A. _____

   B. _____

3. How do you hold the ear for an otoscopic examination on an adult?

   _____

   _____

4. Label the following diagram of the tympanic membrane:

   annulus

   handle of the malleus

   junction of incus and stapes

   light reflex

   pars flaccida

   pars tensa

   short process of the malleus

   umbo

   Is this a diagram of the right or left tympanic membrane? How can you tell?

   _____

5. How do you perform the following tests? Describe normal results.

   Voice-whisper test _____

   _____

   _____

   Weber test _____

   _____

   _____

   Rinne test _____

   _____

   _____

6. Label the following diagram for the frontal, maxillary, and ethmoid sinuses:

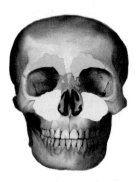

Where are the sphenoid sinuses located?

7. How and why would you transilluminate the sinuses?

_____

_____

_____

_____

8. Where are the salivary glands and their ducts located in the mouth?

Parotid _____

_____

Sublingual _____

_____

Submandibular _____

_____

9. Locate the following anatomical structures on the diagram of the mouth.

anterior pillar
gingiva
palatine tonsil
posterior pharynx
posterior pillar
soft palate
Stensen's duct
uvula
Wharton's duct

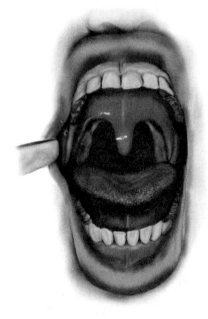

10. **ROS (Review of Systems).** Ask your patient or lab partner the following questions:

    Have you had any injuries or surgery to the ears, nose, mouth, or throat?

    _____

    Do you have frequent colds, sore throat, or allergies?

    _____

    Do you have frequent ear infections or tonsilitis?

    _____

    Do you have any ringing, vertigo, or hearing loss?

    _____

    Do you have any ear pain or discharge?

    _____

    Do you have any sinus pain or sinusitis?

    _____

    Do you have frequent nosebleeds or nasal discharge?

    _____

    Do you have any sores in nose or mouth?

    _____

    Do you have bleeding gums or difficulty chewing?

    _____

    Do you have loose or missing teeth?

    _____

    When was your last dental exam and what is your usual dental care?

    _____

11. **Physical Exam.** *(Equipment: Otoscope, tuning fork, nasal speculum, penlight, tongue blade, gauze square, gloves.)* Follow the physical assessment guidelines in your text to complete the following information:

    Ears
    Auditory screening
      Voice-whisper test   _____
      Tuning fork tests   _____
        Weber test   _____
        Rinne test   _____

External ear
    Inspection   _____
    Palpation   _____
Otoscopic assessment   _____
                                _____
                                _____

Nose

External inspection   _____
Patency   _____
Internal inspection   _____

Sinuses

Inspection   _____
Palpation and percussion   _____

Mouth and Throat

Mouth
    Breath   _____
    Lips
        Inspection   _____
        Palpation   _____
    Tongue   _____
    Buccal mucosa   _____
    Gums   _____
    Teeth   _____
    Palate   _____
Throat   _____
                                _____

Advanced Technique

Transillumination of the sinuses   _____

12. How do you assess cranial nerves IX, X, and XII?

_____

_____

_____

_____

_____

13. Identify several risk factors for oral cancer.

    A. _____

    B. _____

    C. _____

    D. _____

    E. _____

14. You are examining a 2-year-old child who has been crying and pulling on his ear. His mother thinks he has another middle ear infection. What other symptoms might he experience with otitis media?

    _____

    _____

    _____

    What findings would you anticipate during the physical examination?

    _____

    _____

    _____

    List several risk factors for otitis media.

    _____

    _____

    _____

15. Describe findings that might be noted in a patient with poor oral hygiene.

    _____

    _____

    _____

16. You are examining the ears, nose, mouth, and throat of an elderly patient. What common problems are often noted in hearing and taste sensation of the elderly?

    _____

    _____

    _____

    Describe typical changes that occur in the ears and mouth with aging. How might these changes affect the nutrition status of the elderly patient?

    _____

    _____

    _____

    _____

    _____

Self-Assessment Quiz

1. Lucky you! Your patient has a normal eardrum; please describe it briefly.

   _____

   _____

   _____

   _____

   _____

2. Sorry, your patient now has a conductive hearing loss on the left side. What results will each of the following tests give?

   Weber test: _____

   Rinne test: _____

3. Label each of the following normal or abnormal.

   _____ Visible peripheral blood vessels on tympanic membrane

   _____ Light reflex in right ear at 7:00

   _____ Tympanic membrane looks shiny

   _____ No lateralization of sound with the Weber test

   _____ Tympanic membrane moves when patient blows against resistance

4. The technique of shining a light through the maxillary sinus to elicit a glow is called

   _____.

5. Here's a challenge: Which of the following are usually *benign* oral conditions?

oral hairy leukoplakia	angular cheilosis	torus palatinus	Fordyce's spots
candidiasis	scrotal tongue	fibroma	vincent's stomatitis
torus mandibularis	xerostomia	leukoplakia	hemangioma (of the tongue)

6. The primary site of oral cancer is _____.

Lab Practice for Breasts and Regional Nodes

Learning Objectives

1. Locate anatomical structures of the breasts and regional nodes.
2. Conduct a review of systems (ROS) for the breasts.
3. Demonstrate a physical assessment of the breasts and regional nodes.
4. Describe a technique for breast self-examination.
5. Identify and describe characteristics of common breast masses.

Reading Assignment

Before beginning this lab assignment, please read Chapter 14, Breasts and Regional Nodes, in *Health Assessment & Physical Examination* (3rd ed.) by Mary Ellen Zator Estes.

Key Terms

Please define the following terms:

acini _____

_____

alveoli (of the breast) _____

_____

areola _____

_____

augmentation mammoplasty _____

_____

axillary nodes _____

_____

breasts _____

_____

colostrum _____

_____

Cooper's ligaments_____

_____

ductal lavage _____

_____

ectodermal galactic band_____

_____

granulomatous reaction (in the breast) _____

_____

gynecomastia _____ _____

_____

lactiferous ducts _____

_____

lobes (of the breast) _____

_____

lobules (of the breast) _____

_____

lymphatic drainage _____

_____

mastectomy_____

_____

milk line _____

_____

Montgomery's tubercles _____

_____

nipple _____

_____

Paget's disease_____

_____

peau d'orange _____

_____

retromammary adipose tissue _____

_____

supernumerary nipples _____

_____

tail of Spence _____

_____

Laboratory Activities

1. On your patient or lab partner, locate the following four groups of axillary nodes:

   central axillary nodes (midaxillary)
   pectoral (anterior)
   subscapular (posterior)
   brachial (lateral)

   Locate the supraclavicular and infraclavicular lymph nodes.

2. Label the following items on the diagram:

   areola
   Cooper's ligament
   glandular tissue
   lactiferous duct
   lobes
   nipple
   pectoralis major muscle

3. At what developmental stage (sexual maturity rating) do these changes occur?

   _____ Height spurt ends
   _____ Menses begins, breast and areola enlarge
   _____ Nipple protrudes, areola flush with the breast
   _____ Height spurt begins, areola enlarges
   _____ Nipple is small, slightly raised
   _____ Height spurt peaks
   _____ Nipple and breast form a small mound

   A. preadolescent
   B. early adolescent
   C. adolescent
   D. late adolescent
   E. adult

4. What are some techniques that can make your patient more comfortable for the breast examination?

   _____
   _____
   _____
   _____

5. List at least six risk factors for breast cancer.

   A. _____
   B. _____
   C. _____
   D. _____
   E. _____
   F. _____

6. **ROS (Review of Systems).** Ask your patient or lab partner the following questions:

   Have you had any trauma, injury, or surgery to your breasts?

   _____

   Are there changes in your breasts during your menstrual cycle?

   _____

   Do you have any pain, tenderness, or burning in your breasts?

   _____

   Do you have any rash, discharge, lumps, dimpling, or swelling?

   _____

   Are you pregnant or breastfeeding? When was your last menstrual period?

   _____

   Is there a hx of breast disease (yours or family)?

   _____

   When was your last breast exam by MD, CNP, or CNM? When was your last mammogram?

   _____

   Do you perform BSE? What technique do you use? How often do you perform BSE?

   _____

7. **Physical Exam.** *(Equipment: Towel, drape, small centimeter ruler, teaching aid for breast self-examination.)* Follow the physical assessment guidelines in your text to complete the following information:

   Inspection

   Color _____

   Vascularity _____

   Thickening/edema _____

   Size and symmetry _____

   Contour _____

   Lesions/masses _____

   Discharge _____

   Palpation

   Supraclavicular lymph nodes _____

   Infraclavicular lymph nodes _____

   Breasts (patient sitting) _____

   _____

   _____

Axillary lymph nodes   _____

Breasts (patient supine)   _____

_____

8. If you note a mass in your patient's breast, what characteristics do you need to evaluate or describe?

_____

_____

_____

_____

_____

9. If you detect a lump, how can you distinguish between a cyst (benign breast disease), a fibroadenoma, and carcinoma?

Cyst _____

_____

Fibroadenoma _____

_____

Carcinoma _____

_____

10. Using the abbreviation *BSE*, describe how you would teach breast self-examination. Include a pattern for systematic palpation and frequency/timing information.

_____

_____

_____

_____

_____

11. Your patient has just turned 40 years old. How often should the following tests be performed?

Mammogram _____

Physical examination _____

Breast self-examination _____

12. List some of the changes that occur in the breast with aging. How would these changes affect the breast examination?

_____

_____

_____

_____

Self-Assessment Quiz

1. You have discovered a lump in your patient's right breast. What characteristics would you include in your description? (List at least five.)

   A. _____

   B. _____

   C. _____

   D. _____

   E. _____

2. Which of the following characteristics are more likely to be true for a malignancy than for a cyst or fibroadenoma?

   A. most common after age 50

   B. usually mobile

   C. usually nontender

   D. soft to firm consistency

   E. well-defined border

   F. erythema may be present

   G. associated with retraction and dimpling

   H. round or ovoid

3. Which of the following are risk factors for breast cancer?

   A. over age 50

   B. obesity

   C. nulliparous

   D. estrogen therapy

   E. first baby after 30

   F. lives in urban area

   G. maternal hx of breast CA

   H. higher education

   I. atypical hyperplasia

   J. American

   K. early menarche

   L. increased alcohol intake

4. True or false?

   ☐ T ☐ F Males need a clinical breast examination every 1 to 3 years.

   ☐ T ☐ F Breasts normally feel granular in the elderly patient.

   ☐ T ☐ F Nipple discharge may be caused by tranquilizers and oral contraceptives.

   ☐ T ☐ F Supernumerary nipples may be pathologically significant.

   ☐ T ☐ F Palpable lymph nodes that are more than one centimeter and immobile are usually normal.

5. Which technique is being performed in each of the following pictures?

   A. _____   B. _____   C. _____

Lab Practice for Thorax and Lungs

Learning Objectives

1. Locate anatomical landmarks of the thorax and lungs.
2. Conduct a review of systems (ROS) for the respiratory system.
3. Differentiate normal and abnormal breath sounds.
4. Demonstrate appropriate physical assessment techniques.

Reading Assignment

Before beginning this lab assignment, please read Chapter 15, Thorax and Lungs, in *Health Assessment & Physical Examination* (3rd ed.) by Mary Ellen Zator Estes.

Key Terms

Please define the following terms:

adventitious breath sound _____

_____

agonal respirations _____

_____

air trapping _____

_____

alveoli (of the lung) _____

_____

angle of Louis _____

_____

anterior axillary line _____

_____

apex (of the lung)_____

_____

apnea _____

_____

apneustic respirations _____

_____

ataxic respirations _____

_____

barrel chest _____

_____

base (of the lung) _____

_____

Biot's respirations _____

_____

bradypnea _____

_____

bronchial breath sound _____

_____

bronchophony _____

_____

bronchovesicular breath sound _____

_____

Cheyne-Stokes respirations _____

_____

coarse crackle _____

_____

costal angle _____

_____

costal margin_____

_____

cough_____

_____

crepitus _____

_____

diaphragmatic excursion _____

_____

dyspnea _____

_____

egophony _____

_____

eupnea_____

_____

false ribs _____

_____

fine crackle _____

_____

fissure _____

_____

floating ribs _____

_____

hyperpnea _____

_____

intercostal space _____

_____

interpleural space _____

_____

Kussmaul's respirations _____

_____

kyphosis _____

_____

manubriosternal junction _____

_____

manubrium _____

_____

mediastinum _____

_____

midaxillary line _____

_____

midclavicular line _____

_____

midspinal line _____

_____

midsternal line _____

_____

orthopnea _____

_____

parietal pleura _____

_____

pectus carinatum _____

_____

pectus excavatum _____

_____

pleura _____

_____

pleural friction fremitus _____

_____

pleural friction rub _____

_____

posterior axillary line _____

_____

rhonchal fremitus _____

_____

scapular line _____

_____

scoliosis _____

_____

sibilant wheeze _____

_____

sighing _____

_____

sonorous wheeze _____

_____

sputum _____

_____

sternal angle _____

_____

stridor _____

_____

suprasternal notch _____

_____

tachypnea _____

_____

tactile fremitus _____

_____

thoracic expansion _____

_____

true ribs _____

_____

tubular breath sound _____

_____

tussive fremitus _____

_____

vertebral line _____

_____

vertebra prominens _____

_____

vertebrosternal ribs _____

_____

vesicular breath sound _____

_____

visceral pleura _____

_____

vocal fremitus _____

_____

voice sounds _____

_____

whispered pectoriloquy _____

_____

xiphoid process _____

_____

Laboratory Activities

1. Label the following items on the diagram:

   alveoli
   diaphragm
   epiglottis
   larynx
   main bronchus
   mainstem bronchus
   mediastinum
   respiratory bronchiole
   secondary bronchus
   trachea

   Outline and label the
   lobes of the lungs.

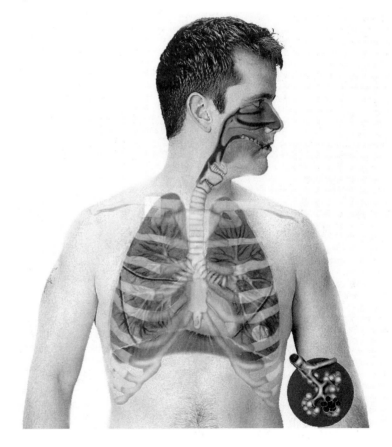

2. Where do the lung apices extend:

   Anteriorly?_____
   Posteriorly? _____

At what level is the lower border of the lung:

Anteriorly at the MCL? _____

Posteriorly on inspiration? _____

Posteriorly on expiration? _____

3. Locate the following thoracic anatomical landmarks on your patient or lab partner:

costal margin	midaxillary line	posterior axillary line
costal angle	xiphoid process	vertebral line
suprasternal notch	midsternal line	vertebra prominens
manubrium of sternum	midclavicular line	spinous process of T1
Angle of Louis	anterior axillary line	

4. What is the normal shape of the thorax? How do you determine the ratio of the AP diameter to the transverse diameter?

    _____

    _____

    _____

    _____

    The normal costal angle is: _____

5. Describe the three normal breath sounds and where they are normally heard.

Breath Sound	Description	Location
Bronchial		
Bronchovesicular		
Vesicular		

6. **ROS (Review of Systems).** Ask your patient or lab partner the following questions:

    Do you have any hx of lung diseases or surgery?

    _____

    Do you have any SOB or chest pain?

    _____

    Do you have any coughing?

    _____

Do you have asthma, allergies, or frequent URIs?

_____

Have you had any change in sputum or any blood-tinged sputum?

_____

Do you have any problems sleeping?

_____

When was your last TB test/chest x-ray? What were the results?

_____

Are you smoking now or did you previously smoke?

_____

8. **Physical Exam.** *(Equipment: Stethoscope, watch with a second hand, centimeter ruler or tape measure, washable marker.)* Follow the physical assessment guidelines in your text to complete the following information:

Inspection

Shape of thorax	normal adult, wider from side to side
Symmetry of chest wall	shoulders same height, no masses
Presence of superficial veins	none visible
Costal angle	
Angle of the ribs	
Intercostal spaces	
Muscles of respiration	
Respirations	
Rate	22 breaths per min
Pattern	
Depth	not exaggerated, effortless
Symmetry	rises and falls in unison
Audibility	cannot hear
Patient position	breaths comfortably
Mode of breathing	through nose
Sputum	none

Palpation

General palpation	
Pulsations	none
Masses	none
Thoracic tenderness	none
Crepitus	none

Thoracic expansion   3-5cm

Tactile fremitus   buzzing

Tracheal position _____

Percussion

General percussion _____

Diaphragmatic excursion _____

Auscultation

General auscultation _____

_____

Breath sounds _____

_____

Voice sounds _____

_____

Advanced Techniques

Locating the site of a fractured rib _____

Forced expiratory time _____

8. How do you assess diaphragmatic excursion? What are normal findings?

_____
_____
_____
_____
_____

9. Your patient has consolidation due to pneumonia. How would you assess each of the following, and what would you expect to find?

Tactile fremitus _____
_____

Bronchophony _____
_____

Egophony _____
_____

Whispered pectoriloquy _____
_____

10. What is the difference between abnormal and adventitious breath sounds?

_____
_____
_____
_____

Describe the six adventitious breath sounds:

	Respiratory Phase	Timing	Description	Etiology
Fine crackle				
Coarse crackle				
Sonorous wheeze				
Sibilant wheeze				
Pleural friction rub				
Stridor				

Which three adventitious breath sounds do not clear with coughing?

A. _____

B. _____

C. _____

11. Complete the following chart comparing a patient with a pulmonary edema to a patient with congestive heart failure (CHF).

	Pulmonary Edema	CHF
Shape of thorax		
Skin color		
Clubbing		
Capillary refill		
Retractions/bulging		

	Pulmonary Edema	**CHF**
Tactile fremitus		
Tracheal position		
Percussion		
Adventitious sounds		

12. Which changes in the respiratory system of your elder patients make them more susceptible to pneumonia?

_____

_____

_____

_____

_____

_____

_____

What risk factors are more probable for patients in a long-term care setting?

_____

_____

_____

_____

_____

Self-Assessment Quiz

1. Fill in the blanks:

   A. The normal breath sound heard over the periphery of the lung fields is _____.

   B. The three stimuli for breathing are _____.

   C. Nailbed clubbing indicates _____.

   D. Subcutaneous emphysema is also called _____.

2. Match each of the following terms with the correct definition:

_____ Muffled, indistinct voice sounds on auscultation

_____ Low-pitched, snoring adventitious sound

_____ Adventitious lung sound, coarse and grating

_____ Abnormal fluid between the layers of the pleura

_____ Collapsed, deflated section of alveoli

_____ Level of the second rib

_____ Palpable vibration over the chest wall when the patient speaks

A. tactile fremitus

B. pleural effusion

C. angle of Louis

D. atelectasis

E. bronchophony

F. friction rub

G. sonorous wheeze

3. Name each of the following abnormal respiratory patterns.

A. _____

C. _____

B. _____

D. _____

4. Label each of the following as normal or abnormal.

_____ Patient A: Tactile fremitus more pronounced at T1 and T2

_____ Patient B: Level of the diaphragm on inspiration at T10

_____ Patient C: Diaphragmatic excursion of 3 cm

_____ Patient D: Peripheral breath sounds that are high pitched with a blowing/hollow quality

_____ Patient E: Barrel chest and kyphosis in an older patient

5. Match each of the following findings with the probable condition:

_____ Absent breath sounds

_____ Hyperresonance

_____ Absent voice sounds

_____ Rust-colored or blood-tinged sputum

_____ Pleural friction rub

_____ Pink sputum

_____ Fine crackles

_____ Increased tactile fremitus

A. pneumonia

B. asthma

C. pulmonary edema

D. COPD

6. Risk factors for lung cancer include:

_____

_____

Lab Practice for Heart and Peripheral Vasculature

Chapter 16

Learning Objectives

1. Identify anatomical structures and landmarks of the chest and periphery.
2. Conduct a review of systems (ROS) for the cardiovascular system.
3. Demonstrate appropriate physical assessment techniques.
4. Differentiate normal and abnormal findings.

Reading Assignment

Before beginning this lab assignment, please read Chapter 16, Heart and Peripheral Vasculature, in *Health Assessment & Physical Examination* (3rd ed.) by Mary Ellen Zator Estes.

Key Terms

Please define the following terms:

afterload _____

_____

Allen test _____

_____

angina _____

_____

apex (of the heart) _____

_____

atrial kick_____

_____

atrioventricular (A-V) node _____

_____

atrioventricular (A-V) valves _____

_____

baroreceptors _____

_____

base (of the heart) _____

_____

bruit _____

_____

cardiomegaly _____

_____

click _____

_____

crescendo _____

_____

decrescendo _____

_____

diastole _____

_____

edema _____

_____

electrocardiogram (EKG) _____

_____

gallop _____

_____

heave _____

_____

holosystolic _____

_____

Homan's sign _____

_____

hyperkinetic _____

_____

hypokinetic _____

_____

infarction (myocardial) _____

_____

insufficiency _____

_____

ischemia (myocardial) _____

_____

isoelectric line _____

_____

lift _____

_____

orthostatic hypotension _____

_____

pallor _____

_____

palpitation _____
_____

pansystolic _____
_____

parietal pericardium _____
_____

pericarditis _____
_____

precordium _____
_____

preload _____
_____

pulsus paradoxus _____
_____

regurgitation _____
_____

septum _____
_____

sinoatrial (S-A) node _____
_____

snap _____
_____

stenosis _____
_____

syncope _____
_____

systole _____
_____

thrill _____
_____

tilts _____
_____

visceral pericardium _____
_____

Laboratory Activities

1. Label the following items on the diagram of the heart:

    aorta
    aortic valve
    inferior vena cava
    left atrium
    left pulmonary artery
    left ventricle
    mitral valve
    pulmonary valve
    Pulmonary veins
    right atrium
    right pulmonary artery
    right ventricle
    superior vena cava
    tricuspid valve

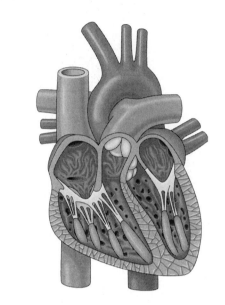

2. Label the following cardiac landmarks on the diagram:

    A = aortic area
    P = pulmonic area
    E = Erb's point
    T = tricuspid area
    M = mitral area
    B = base of the heart
    X = apex of the heart

    Identify the angle of Louis.

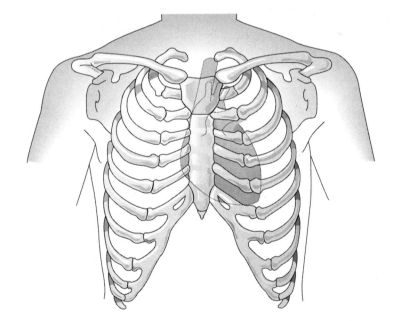

3. Locate the following anatomical landmarks on your patient or lab partner:

   suprasternal notch
   angle of Louis
   Right and left second ICS
   cardiac landmarks: aortic, pulmonic, Erb's point, tricuspid, mitral
   peripheral pulses: temporal, carotid, brachial, radial, femoral, popliteal, posterior tibial, dorsalis
   pedis

4. Identify and differentiate S_1 and S_2. Where is each sound heard loudest to auscultation?

   _____

   _____

   _____

   _____

   _____

5. Describe S_3 and S_4. When in the cardiac cycle are these heard?

   _____

   _____

   _____

   _____

   _____

   What is the significance of each of these heart sounds?

   _____

   _____

   _____

6. While assessing a high school student for a sports physical, you detect a physiologic splitting of
   the S_2. Where would you auscultate the split S_2, and what causes it?

   _____

   _____

   _____

   _____

   _____

7. How would you calculate the target heart rate for a patient who is 25? A patient who is 60?

   _____

   _____

8. How do you inspect for jugular venous pressure? What are normal values?

_____

_____

_____

_____

_____

9. What is the difference between a thrill and a heave?

_____

_____

_____

10. **ROS (Review of Systems).** Ask your patient or lab partner the following questions:

    Have you had any hx of heart disease, murmurs, rheumatic fever?

    _____

    Do you have any bleeding disorders, DM, HTN?

    _____

    Have you had any hx of chest trauma or surgery?

    _____

    Do you have any chest pain, SOB, or coughing?

    _____

    Do you tire easily? Awaken at night to urinate?

    _____

    Do you have any sores or lesions on your arms or legs?

    _____

    Do you have any leg cramps, pain, or swelling of your feet or legs?

    _____

    Do you exercise (activity, duration, and frequency)?

    _____

    Have you had an EKG, chest x-ray, or tests for cholesterol? What were the results?

    _____

11. **Physical Exam.** *(Equipment: Stethoscope, sphygmomanometer, watch with second hand, tape measure.)* Follow the physical assessment guidelines in your text to complete the following information:

Assessment of the Precordium

Inspection

    Aortic area   _____

    Pulmonic area   _____

    Midprecordial area   _____

    Tricuspid area   _____

    Mitral area   _____

Palpation

    Aortic area   _____

    Pulmonic area   _____

    Midprecordial area   _____

    Tricuspid area   _____

    Mitral area   _____

Auscultation

    Aortic area

    Pulmonic area

    Midprecordial area

    Tricuspid area

    Mitral area

    Mitral and tricuspid area (S_3)

    Mitral and tricuspid area (S_4)

    Murmurs

    Pericardial friction rub

    Prosthetic heart valves

Assessment of the Peripheral Vasculature

Inspection of the jugular venous
       pressure

Inspection of the hepatojugular
       reflux

Palpation and auscultation of
       arterial pulses
       (See figure in question 12.)

Inspection and palpation of
       peripheral perfusion

    Peripheral pulse

    Color

    Clubbing

Capillary refill _____

Skin temperature _____

Edema _____

Ulcerations _____

Skin texture _____

Hair distribution _____

Palpation of the epitrochlear node _____

Advanced Techniques

Orthostatic hypotension

Assessment _____

Assessing for pulsus paradoxus _____

Assessing the venous system

    Homan's sign _____

    Manual compression _____

    Retrograde filling, or

        Trendelenburg test _____

Assessing the arterial system

    Pallor _____

    Color return and venous

        filling time _____

    Allen test _____

Assistive Devices Used

_____

_____

_____

12. Document the amplitude of the peripheral pulses using the stick figure.

13. Identify any cardiac risk factors for your patient or lab partner.

    _____

    _____

    _____

14. Describe the assessment for orthostatic hypotension.

    _____

    _____

    _____

    _____

    _____

15. List the seven characteristics used to describe a murmur.

    A. _____

    B. _____

    C. _____

    D. _____

    E. _____

    F. _____

    G. _____

16. How would you perform the Allen test? Why would this technique be performed?

    _____

    _____

    _____

    _____

17. What are the warning signs of potential cardiovascular problems?

    _____

    _____

    _____

    _____

    _____

18. You are performing an admission physical exam on an 84-year-old resident at a long-term care facility. What are expected alterations in the cardiovascular system for this patient?

    _____

    _____

    _____

    _____

    _____

What will you include for a thorough assessment of this patient's peripheral vasculature?

_____

_____

_____

_____

During your assessment, you note ulcerations on the patient's lower extremities. How would you determine if they are arterial or venous ulcerations?

_____

_____

_____

_____

_____

_____

_____

19. What effect can each of the following have on the cardiovascular system of the elderly patient?

COPD _____

Obesity _____

Smoking _____

Osteoporosis _____

Diabetes mellitus _____

Self-Assessment Quiz

1. What is the normal pathway of blood flow through the heart (including valves)?

_____

_____

_____

_____

2. True or false?

☐ **T** ☐ **F** S_1 represents the closing of the aortic and pulmonic (semilunar) valves.

☐ **T** ☐ **F** S_2 is heard loudest at the base of the heart.

☐ **T** ☐ **F**   The apex is closer to the 4th/5th ICS; the base is closer to the 2nd ICS.

☐ **T** ☐ **F**   Erb's point is auscultated at the 4th ICS left sternal border.

☐ **T** ☐ **F**   A JVP less than 4 cm is considered normal.

☐ **T** ☐ **F**   The sound of an S_4 is represented by the word "Kentucky."

☐ **T** ☐ **F**   A murmur graded V/VI can be heard with the diaphragm held off the chest.

☐ **T** ☐ **F**   Increased jugular vein distention may be seen in right-sided heart failure.

☐ **T** ☐ **F**   Blanching in the extremities followed by cyanosis is seen in Raynaud's disease.

3. Match the following findings:

   _____ Noted at 5th ICS, left midclavicular line   A. thrill

   _____ High-pitched, multiphasic, scratchy   B. murmur

   _____ Final phase of diastole   C. mitral valve murmur

   _____ Turbulent blood flow   D. heart failure

   _____ Often associated with an S_3 E. pericardial friction rub

   _____ Noted with palpation   F. atrial kick

4. What are the risk factors for cardiac disease? Circle those that are fixed.

   _____

   _____

   _____

   _____

5. Match the cardiovascular disorder to its common findings:

   _____ Anorexia, fatigue, arthralgia, petechiae   A. pulmonary embolus

   _____ Severe pain, paresthesia, intermittent claudication   B. CHF (left-sided)

   _____ SOB, angina, dysrhythmias, nausea, diaphoresis   C. CHF (right-sided)

   _____ Diaphoresis, rales, S_3, anxiety, fatigue   D. endocarditis

   _____ Sudden onset, sharp or stabbing pain, anxiety   E. atherosclerosis

   _____ Dependent edema, hepatomegaly, weight gain   F. myocardial infarction

   _____ Angina, MI, dysrhythmias, sudden cardiac death   G. peripheral vascular disease

Lab Practice for Abdomen

Learning Objectives

1. Locate anatomical structures of the abdomen.
2. Conduct a review of systems (ROS) for the abdomen.
3. Demonstrate appropriate physical assessment techniques.
4. Differentiate normal and abnormal findings.
5. Describe assessment techniques for abdominal pain and ascites.

Reading Assignment

Before beginning this lab assignment, please read Chapter 17, Abdomen, in *Health Assessment & Physical Examination* (3rd ed.) by Mary Ellen Zator Estes.

Key Terms

Please define the following terms:

ascites _____

_____

ballottement _____

_____

borborygmi _____

_____

caput medusae _____

_____

Cullen's sign _____

_____

cutaneous hypersensitivity _____

_____

eructation _____

_____

flatulence _____

_____

fluid wave _____

_____

hematemesis _____

_____

iliopsoas muscle test _____

_____

linea alba _____

_____

McBurney's point _____

_____

Murphy's sign _____

_____

obturator sign _____

_____

puddle sign _____

_____

rebound tenderness _____

_____

Rovsing's sign _____

_____

shifting dullness _____

_____

striae _____

_____

venous hum_____

_____

Laboratory Activities

1. What is the sequence for examination of the abdomen? Give the rationale.

   _____

   _____

   What strategies can increase your patient's comfort during the examination?

   _____

   _____

   _____

   _____

   _____

2. Label the following items on the diagram:

   appendix
   ascending colon
   bladder
   descending colon
   gallbladder
   inguinal ligament
   liver
   pancreas
   spleen
   stomach
   transverse colon

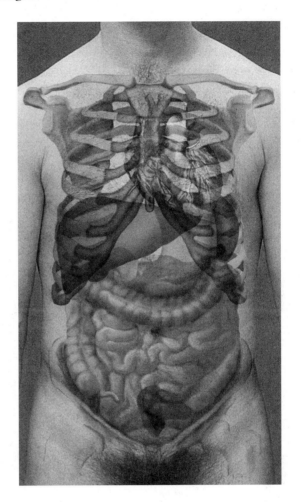

3. List the primary functions of each of the following:

   stomach _____
   small intestine _____
   large intestine _____
   liver _____
   gallbladder_____
   pancreas _____
   spleen _____
   kidneys _____

4. Locate the following anatomical landmarks on your patient or lab partner:

xiphoid process	abdominal midline	rectus abdominis muscle
costal margin	symphysis pubis	costovertebral angle
umbilicus	anterior superior iliac spine	linea alba
inguinal ligament	abdominal quadrants	12th rib

5. What is the predominate sound heard with percussion of the abdomen? Why?

_____

_____

6. Mark on the diagram where you auscultate for bruits.

   A = abdominal aorta

   R = renal arteries

   I = iliac arteries

   F = femoral arteries

7. **ROS (Review of Systems).** Ask your patient or lab partner the following questions:

   Do you have a hx of GI disease or surgery?

_____

   Do you have any hx of abdominal trauma?

_____

   Do you have a hx of eating disorders?

_____

   Do you have any abdominal pain, nausea, vomiting, or heartburn?

_____

   Have you had a change in appetite or intolerance to foods?

_____

   Do you have diarrhea, distension, or constipation?

_____

Do you have excessive belching or flatulence?

_____

Do you have any difficulty swallowing?

_____

Do you have any dysuria or nocturia?

_____

What is your usual stool pattern (frequency, color, consistency)?

_____

Have you traveled recently?

_____

What was your previous 24-hour diet hx?

_____

8. **Physical Exam.** *(Equipment: Stethoscope, small centimeter ruler, drape, tangential lighting, marking pencil, sterile safety pin.)* Follow the physical assessment guidelines in your text to complete the following information:

Inspection

Contour _____

Symmetry _____

Rectus abdominis muscles _____

Pigmentation and color _____

Scars _____

Striae _____

Respiratory movement _____

Masses or nodules _____

Visible peristalsis _____

Pulsation _____

Umbilicus _____

Auscultation

Bowel sounds _____

Vascular sounds _____

Venous hum _____

Friction rubs _____

Percussion

General percussion _____

Liver span _____

Liver descent _____

Spleen _____

Stomach _____

Fist percussion

    Kidney _____

    Liver _____

Bladder _____

Palpation

Light palpation _____

Abdominal muscle guarding _____

Deep palpation _____

Liver

    Bimanual or hook method _____

Spleen _____

Kidneys _____

Aorta _____

Bladder _____

Inguinal lymph nodes _____

Advanced Techniques

Scratch test _____

Percussion for ascites

    Shifting dullness _____

    Puddle sign _____

Fluid wave _____

Murphy's sign _____

Rebound tenderness _____

Rovsing's sign _____

Cutaneous hypersensitivity _____

Iliopsoas muscle test _____

Obturator muscle test _____

Ballottement _____

9. How do you estimate liver span?

_____

_____

_____

_____

_____

The normal liver span for an adult at the MCL is _____.

10. What are the possible causes of abdominal distension?

11. Describe three methods used to assess for ascites.

    A.

    B.

    C.

12. When should you avoid palpation of an area?

13. What are five advanced techniques that can assess for appendicitis?

Technique	**Description**
A.	
B.	
C.	
D.	
E.	

14. Risk factors for liver cancer include:

    A.   D.

    B.   E.

    C.   F.

15. What changes occur in the abdomen with aging?

_____
_____
_____
_____
_____

16. If your elderly patient complains of a change in bowel habits, what causes should be considered?

_____
_____
_____
_____
_____

What factors put the elderly patient at risk for functional incontinence?

_____
_____
_____

Self-Assessment Quiz

1. The abdomen is located between the _____ and the _____.

2. In which quadrant is each of the following located?

_____ Liver   _____ Spleen   A. right upper

_____ Stomach   _____ Kidneys   B. right lower

_____ Appendix   _____ Sigmoid colon   C. left upper

_____ Gallbladder   _____ Descending colon D. left lower

_____ Duodenum   _____ Body of the pancreas

3. Will you use the diaphragm or the bell of your stethoscope to auscultate these?

_____ Carotid arteries   _____ Femoral artery bruit

_____ Bowel sounds   _____ Voice sounds (lungs)

_____ Thyroid gland   _____ Venous hum

_____ Lungs   _____ Heart

4. Label each of the following normal or abnormal.

_____ A visible aortic pulsation

_____ Positive borborygmi

_____ Aortic width of 5 cm

_____ Small movable inguinal nodes

_____ Hypoactive bowel sounds

_____ Liver span of 7 cm at the midclavicular line

_____ Negative Rovsing's sign

_____ Small fluid wave

5. What are the "Seven Fs" of abdominal distension?

A. _____

B. _____

C. _____

D. _____

E. _____

F. _____

G. _____

6. "Where does it hurt?"

A. Pain originating in an organ may be experienced in another area. This is called _____.

B. If the patient has abdominal pain, that area should be palpated _____.

C. Before beginning the assessment, ask the patient to _____ to elicit a sharp twinge of pain in the involved area.

D. Lightly palpate the rectus muscles during expiration to determine the presence of

_____.

E. While performing abdominal palpation, observe the patient's face for

_____.

F. Murphy's sign is positive with inflammation of the _____.

G. Applying firm pressure to the abdomen and quickly releasing it may produce _____ in the presence of peritoneal irritation.

H. Pain in the RLQ may indicate _____.

Lab Practice for Musculoskeletal System

Learning Objectives

1. Locate anatomical structures of the musculoskeletal system.
2. Conduct a review of systems (ROS) for the musculoskeletal system.
3. Demonstrate a physical assessment of the musculoskeletal system.
4. Describe abnormal gait patterns.

Reading Assignment

Before beginning this lab assignment, please read Chapter 18, Musculoskeletal System, in *Health Assessment & Physical Examination* (3rd ed.) by Mary Ellen Zator Estes.

Key Terms

Please define the following terms:

acromegaly _____

_____

appendicular skeleton _____

_____

atrophy _____

_____

axial skeleton _____

_____

Bouchard's node _____

_____

bow legs _____

_____

bursae _____

_____

callus _____

_____

corn _____

_____

diaphysis _____

_____

dislocation_____

_____

epimysium_____

_____

epiphyses_____

_____

ganglion_____

_____

genu valgum_____

_____

genu varum_____

_____

goniometer_____

_____

hallux valgus_____

_____

hammertoe_____

_____

Heberden's node_____

_____

hemiparesis_____

_____

hemiplegia_____

_____

hypertrophy_____

_____

hypotonicity_____

_____

joint_____

_____

knock knees_____

_____

kyphosis_____

_____

ligament_____

_____

list_____

_____

lordosis _____

_____

medullary cavity _____

_____

pes cavus _____

_____

pes planus _____

_____

pes valgus _____

_____

pes varus _____

_____

polydactyly _____

_____

scoliosis _____

_____

spasticity _____

_____

subluxation _____

_____

syndactyly _____

_____

synovial effusion _____

_____

tendons _____

_____

thenar eminence _____

_____

Laboratory Activities

1. Label each of the bones on this diagram:

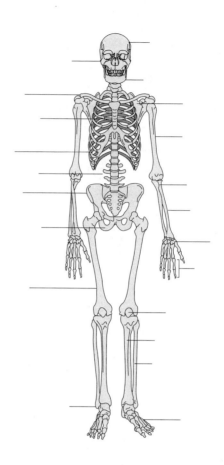

2. Label the following muscles on the diagram:

biceps

brachioradialis

deltoid

external oblique

iliopsoas

masseter

pectoralis major

quadriceps femoris

rectus abdominis

serratus anterior

sternocleidomastoid

temporalis

tibialis anterior

triceps

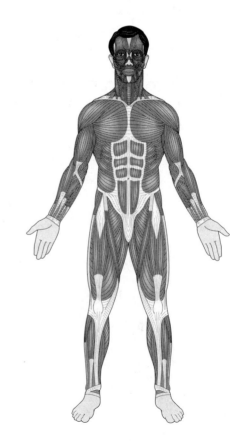

3. Locate the following major bone and muscle structures on your patient or lab partner:

humerus	patella	metatarsals	vertebral column	biceps
ulna	femur	metacarpals	sternum	triceps
radius	fibula	clavicle	trapezius	quadriceps
carpals	tibia	maxilla	gluteus maximus	deltoid
tarsals	mandible	phalanges	rectus abdominis	

4. Which patients require a complete musculoskeletal assessment?

_____

_____

_____

_____

_____

What does a screening, or musculoskeletal mini-assessment, include?

_____

_____

5. Have your patient or lab partner perform these skeletal muscle movements:

flexion	internal rotation	elevation	inversion
extension	external rotation	depression	eversion
abduction	pronation	protraction	dorsiflexion
adduction	supination	retraction	plantar flexion
rotation	opposition	hyperextension	lateral bending
circumduction			

6. Describe two techniques used to assess for carpal tunnel syndrome.

_____

_____

_____

_____

_____

What types of activities might lead to this injury?

_____

_____

7. Describe six range-of-motion movements for the shoulder.

   A. _____

   B. _____

   C. _____

   D. _____

   E. _____

   F. _____

8. **ROS (Review of Systems).** Ask your patient or lab partner the following questions:

   Do you have a hx of broken bones, sprains, dislocations, or other trauma?

   _____

   Do you have any bone or joint deformity?

   _____

   Do you have any joint stiffness, swelling, redness, or pain?

   _____

   Do you have frequent or severe back pain?

   _____

   Do you have any loss of mobility, strength, or endurance?

   _____

   Can you perform all daily activities (lifting, walking, pushing, pulling, etc.)?

   _____

   Do you do any strenuous activities at work, home, or sports?

   _____

   Do you perform any repetitive motion activities for work or hobbies?

   _____

   Do you exercise (type, duration, frequency)?

   _____

9. **Physical Exam.** *(Equipment: Goniometer, cloth measuring tape, sphygmomanometer and blood pressure cuff, washable marker.)* Follow the physical assessment guidelines in your text to complete the following information:

   General Assessment

   Overall appearance   _____

   Posture   _____

   Gait and mobility   _____

   _____

   _____

Inspection

Muscle size and shape   _____

Joint contour and

       periarticular tissue   _____

Palpation

Muscle tone   _____

Joints   _____

Range of Motion   _____

_____

_____

Muscle Strength   _____

_____

Examination of Joints

Temporomandibular joint   _____

Cervical spine   _____

Shoulders   _____

Elbows   _____

Wrists and hands   _____

Hips   _____

Knees   _____

Ankles and feet   _____

Spine   _____

Advanced Techniques

Measuring limb circumference

     using a goniometer   _____

Chvostek's sign (neuroexcitability)   _____

Drop arm test (rotator cuff damage)   _____

Trousseau's sign (neuroexcitability)   _____

Assessing grip strength using a

     blood pressure cuff   _____

Tinel's sign (carpal tunnel syndrome)   _____

Phalen's sign (carpal tunnel syndrome)   _____

Trendelenburg test (hip dislocation)   _____

Measuring limb length   _____

Patrick's test (degenerative joint

     disease in the hip)   _____

Bulge sign (small effusions)   _____

Patellar ballottement (large effusions)   _____

Apley's grinding sign (meniscal tears) _____

McMurray's sign (meniscal tears) _____

Drawer test (cruciate ligaments) _____

Lachman's test (anterior cruciate
ligament) _____

Varus stress test (lateral collateral
ligament) _____

Valgum stress test (medial collateral
ligament) _____

Anterior drawer test (angle sprain) _____

Talar tilt test (ankle sprain) _____

Assessing status of distal limbs
and digits _____

Thompson squeeze test (ruptured
Achilles tendon) _____

Adams forward bend test (scoliosis) _____

Straight leg raising test _____

Lasègue's test (herniated disc) _____

Milgram test (herniated disc) _____

Assistive Devices Used _____

10. Describe the body mechanics of an erect posture and a normal gait.

_____

_____

_____

_____

_____

11. How can you differentiate between osteoarthritis and rheumatoid arthritis?

_____

_____

_____

_____

_____

12. What is the significance of the notation S3/T2/L3?

_____

_____

_____

_____

13. Differentiate findings in scoliosis, kyphosis, and lordosis.

_____

_____

_____

_____

_____

The curvature seen in pregnancy is called _____.

Adolescents are assessed for _____.

The curvature associated with osteoporosis is called _____.

How do you assess for scoliosis?

_____

_____

_____

_____

14. Briefly describe several advanced techniques that can be used to examine the knee.

Technique	Method	Etiology
Bulge sign		
Patellar ballottement		
Apley's grinding sign		
Varus stress test		
Drawer test		
Lachman's test		

15. What are the "Five Ps" of neurovascular deterioration?

A. _____

B. _____

C. _____

D. _____

E. _____

16. What changes might you see in the musculoskeletal system of an elderly female patient?

_____

_____

_____

_____

_____

_____

17. How do age-related changes affect the ability of the elderly patient to perform ADLs?

_____

_____

_____

_____

_____

18. List signs that may indicate elder abuse or neglect.

_____

_____

_____

_____

_____

Self-Assessment Quiz

1. Match the following special techniques:

   _____ Is positive in neuroexcitability

   _____ Detects rotator cuff damage

   _____ Assesses the integrity of the meniscus

   _____ Is positive with a rupture of the Achilles tendon

   _____ Tests for small effusions in the knee

   _____ Detects loose or movable objects in the knee

   _____ Positive in carpal tunnel syndrome

   _____ Detects ankle sprain

   _____ Assesses stability of the anterior cruciate ligament

   A. Phalen's sign

   B. Lachman's test

   C. Trousseau's sign

   D. bulge sign

   E. Apley's grinding sign

   F. Thompson squeeze test

   G. drop arm test

   H. McMurray's sign

   I. talar tilt test

2. Because your patient has "complete ROM against gravity with moderate resistance," you grade this muscle strength as a _____ on a scale of _____.

3. True or false?

   ☐ **T** ☐ **F**   Osteoarthritis may cause joints to appear hot, tender, and painful, with possible deformities.

   ☐ **T** ☐ **F**   Bouchard and Heberden's nodes are findings in rheumatoid arthritis.

   ☐ **T** ☐ **F**   You ask your patient to do a shoulder shrug to test CN XII.

   ☐ **T** ☐ **F**   Rotator cuff damage is assessed in the drop arm test.

   ☐ **T** ☐ **F**   A positive Trendelenburg test indicates hip dislocation.

   ☐ **T** ☐ **F**   Osteoporosis produces uneven shoulders and hip levels that can be detected by having the patient bend over.

4. Match each of the following findings:

   _____ Slow, writhing, twisting movement

   _____ Pes planus

   _____ Visible twitching of muscle fibers

   _____ Genu valgum

   _____ Enlargement of skull, hands, feet, and long bones

   _____ Sudden, rapid muscle spasms in upper body

   _____ Genu varum

   _____ Hallux valgus

   A. knock knees

   B. bow legs

   C. flat foot

   D. bunion

   E. tic

   F. fasciculation

   G. athetosis

   H. acromegaly

5. True or false?

   ☐ **T** ☐ **F**   Festinating is seen in Parkinson's disease.

   ☐ **T** ☐ **F**   An apraxic gait is slow and shuffling.

   ☐ **T** ☐ **F**   Cerebellar ataxia causes the patient to stagger and sway.

   ☐ **T** ☐ **F**   With muscular dystrophy or hip dysplasia, a "waddling" gait may be seen.

   ☐ **T** ☐ **F**   Causes of abnormal gait include muscle weakness, joint deterioration, paralysis, lack of coordination and balance, fatigue, and pain.

6. Label each of these abnormalities of the spine:

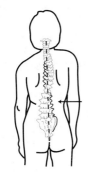 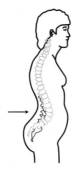 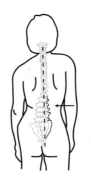 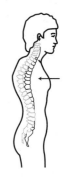

A. _____ B. _____ C. _____ D. _____

7. The test that assesses for a herniated lumbar disc is _____.

Lab Practice for Mental Status and Neurological Techniques

Chapter 19

Learning Objectives

1. Identify structures in the central nervous system.
2. Conduct a review of systems (ROS) for the neurological system.
3. Demonstrate a mental status examination and appropriate physical assessment techniques.
4. Differentiate normal and abnormal findings.

Reading Assignment

Before beginning this lab assignment, please read Chapter 19, Mental Status and Neurological Techniques, in *Health Assessment & Physical Examination* (3rd ed.) by Mary Ellen Zator Estes.

Key Terms

Please define the following terms:

ageusia _____

_____

agnosia _____

_____

agraphia _____

_____

alexia _____

_____

analgesia _____

_____

anesthesia _____

_____

anosmia _____

_____

aphasia _____

_____

aphonia _____

_____

apraxia _____

_____

astereognosis _____

_____

Bell's palsy _____

_____

clonus _____

_____

confabulation _____

_____

constructional apraxia _____

_____

decerebrate rigidity _____

_____

decorticate rigidity _____

_____

dermatome _____

_____

dysarthria _____

_____

dyscalculia _____

_____

dysdiadochokinesia _____

_____

dysesthesia _____

_____

dysmetria _____

_____

dysphonia _____

_____

dyssynergy _____

_____

echolalia _____

_____

Glasgow Coma Scale _____

_____

graphanesthesia _____

_____

graphesthesia _____

_____

hypalgesia _____
_____

hyperalgesia _____
_____

hyperesthesia _____
_____

hypesthesia _____
_____

hypoesthesia _____
_____

hypogeusia _____
_____

neologism _____
_____

paresthesia _____
_____

proprioception _____
_____

seizure _____
_____

stereognosis _____
_____

syncope _____
_____

vertigo _____
_____

Laboratory Activities

1. How do the sympathetic and parasympathetic nervous systems differ?

_____
_____
_____
_____
_____
_____

2. Label the following items on the drawing:

Broca's area
cerebellum
diencephalon
frontal lobe
occipital lobe
parietal lobe
spinal cord
temporal lobe
Wernicke's area

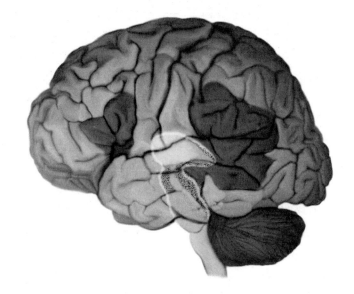

3. What information can you obtain about your patient's mental status and neurological function during the patient interview?

_____
_____
_____
_____

4. Name the three categories of reflexes and give examples of each:

Category	**Examples**

5. What items are included in a neurological screening assessment?

_____
_____
_____
_____
_____

6. Describe an assessment technique for each of the cranial nerves.

CN No.	Name	Assessment Technique
I		
II		
III		
IV		
V		
VI		
VII		
VIII		
IX		
X		
XI		
XII		

7. How could you assess coordination in the upper and lower extremities?

8. **ROS (Review of Systems).** Ask your patient or lab partner the following questions:

Have you had any head or spinal cord injuries?

_____

Have you had any hx of stroke, meningitis, alcoholism, or hypertension?

_____

Do you have any congenital defects?

_____

Have you had any psychiatric illness or emotional disturbance?

_____

Have you had any communicable diseases such as polio, AIDS, syphilis, rickettsial infections?

_____

Have you had any fainting, dizziness, loss of coordination, or weakness?

_____

Do you have any numbness, tingling, or tremors?

_____

Have you had any changes in your vision?

_____

Are you having any memory loss?

_____

Do you have any difficulty with speaking or swallowing?

_____

Are you experiencing chronic or unusual stress?

_____

Are you exposed to environmental or occupational hazards?

_____

9. **Physical Exam.** *(Equipment: Reflex hammer, tuning fork, tongue blade, penlight, cotton-tipped applicators, cotton ball, sterile safety pin, familiar small objects [coins, key, paperclip], vials of odorous materials [coffee, etc.], vials of hot and cold water, vials with solutions for tasting, Snellen chart, pupil gauge.)* Follow the physical assessment guidelines in your text to complete the following information:

Mental Status Assessment

Physical appearance and behavior

   Posture and movements   _____

   Dress, grooming, and

      personal hygiene   _____

   Facial expression   _____

   Affect   _____

Communication   _____

Level of consciousness   _____

Cognitive abilities and mentation

   Cognitive mental status screening   _____

   Attention   _____

   Memory   _____

   Judgment   _____

   Insight   _____

   Spatial perception   _____

   Calculation   _____

   Abstract reasoning   _____

   Thought process and content   _____

   Suicidal ideation   _____

Sensory Assessment

Exteroceptive sensation

   Light touch   _____

   Superficial pain   _____

   Temperature   _____

Proprioceptive sensation

   Motion and position   _____

   Vibration sense   _____

Cortical sensation

   Stereognosis   _____

   Graphesthesia   _____

   Two-point discrimination   _____

   Extinction   _____

Cranial Nerves Assessment

Olfactory nerve (CN I) _____

Optic nerve (CN II)

    Visual acuity _____

    Visual fields _____

    Funduscopic examination _____

Oculomotor nerve (CN III)

    Cardinal fields of gaze _____

    Eyelid elevation _____

    Pupil reactions _____

Trochlear nerve (CN IV)

    Cardinal fields of gaze _____

Trigeminal nerve (CN V)

    Motor component _____

    Sensory component _____

Abducens nerve (CN VI)

    Cardinal fields of gaze _____

Facial nerve (CN VII)

    Motor component _____

    Sensory component _____

Acoustic nerve (CN VIII)

    Cochlear division

        Hearing _____

        Weber test _____

        Rinne test _____

    Vestibular division _____

Glossopharyngeal nerve (CN IX) _____

Vagus nerve (CN X) _____

Spinal accessory nerve (CN XI) _____

Hypoglossal nerve (CN XII) _____

Motor System Assessment

Muscle size _____

Muscle tone _____

Muscle strength _____

Involuntary movements _____

Pronator drift _____

Cerebellar Function

Coordination _____

Station _____

Gait _____

Reflexes

Deep tendon reflexes

   Biceps _____

   Brachioradialis _____

   Triceps _____

   Patellar _____

   Achilles _____

Superficial reflexes

   Abdominal _____

   Plantar _____

   Cremasteric _____

   Bulbocavernosus _____

Pathological reflexes

   Glabellar _____

   Clonus _____

   Babinski _____

Advanced Techniques

Doll's eyes phenomenon _____

Romberg's test _____

Meningeal irritation

   Nuchal rigidity _____

   Kernig's sign _____

   Brudzinski's sign _____

10. Document your findings for the deep tendon reflexes (DTRs) and superficial reflexes on the stick figure.

Complete the grading scale for the DTRs.

0 _____

1+ _____

2+ _____

3+ _____

4+ _____

11. Describe the following techniques for assessment of meningeal irritation.

Kernig's sign _____

_____

Nuchal rigidity _____

_____

Brudzinski's sign _____

_____

12. How would you determine a patient's LOC using the Glasgow Coma Scale?

_____
_____
_____
_____

13. If your patient displays a positive Romberg's test, what is happening?

_____
_____
_____

How would your findings compare for a patient with cerebellar disease and a patient with posterior column disease?

_____
_____
_____

14. Describe possible assessment findings for a patient with Parkinson's disease.

_____
_____
_____
_____

15. What neurological changes in the older patient could contribute to the onset of depression?

_____
_____
_____
_____
_____

16. What assessments for mental status could help differentiate dementia and depression in a patient?

_____
_____
_____

Self-Assessment Quiz

1. Each of the following patients shows an abnormal finding in which cognitive function?

   A. attention   E. spatial perception
   B. memory   F. calculation
   C. judgment   G. abstract reasoning
   D. insight   H. thought process/content

   _____ Patient 1: Can't explain the meaning of "A squeaky wheel gets the grease."

   _____ Patient 2: Gives an inappropriate answer to "What would you do if you saw a house burning?"

   _____ Patient 3: Can't recall a list of three items after a five-minute conversation.

   _____ Patient 4: Has difficulty with serial 7s.

   _____ Patient 5: Displays agnosia and constructional apraxia.

   _____ Patient 6: Uses confabulation when answering.

   _____ Patient 7: Is euphoric.

   _____ Patient 8: Is unable to repeat a given sequence of numbers.

2. Which deep tendon reflexes are shown here?

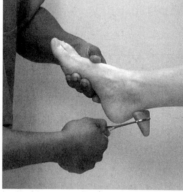
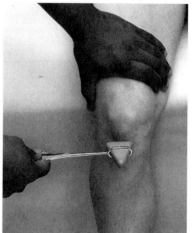

   A. _____   B. _____   C. _____

3. True or false?

 ☐ **T** ☐ **F**   Broca's area is responsible for auditory comprehension.

 ☐ **T** ☐ **F**   The posterior column carries vibration and fine-touch sensations.

 ☐ **T** ☐ **F**   Reflexes are classified as muscle stretch, superficial, or pathological.

 ☐ **T** ☐ **F**   Parasympathetic responses change pupil size and increase urine output.

 ☐ **T** ☐ **F**   The GCS assesses patients on eye opening, verbal response, and reflexes.

 ☐ **T** ☐ **F**   The loss of the doll's eyes phenomenon is found in patients with a low brain stem lesion.

4. "Oh, what nerve . . . " (cranial nerve, that is)?

   Affects strength of trapezius muscles: CN _____

   Allows patient to produce guttural sounds: CN _____

   Ageusia and Bell's palsy are abnormal findings: CN _____

   20/25 OD, 20/20 OS, 20/20 OU: CN _____

   Vertigo would be an abnormal finding: CN _____

   Allows direct and consensual pupil response to light: CN _____

5. What techniques assess for meningeal irritation?

   _____

Lab Practice for Female Genitalia

Learning Objectives

1. Identify anatomical structures of the female genitalia.
2. Conduct a review of systems (ROS) for the genitalia.
3. Demonstrate appropriate physical assessment technique.
4. Differentiate normal and atypical findings.

Reading Assignment

Before beginning this lab assignment, please read Chapter 20, Female Genitalia, in *Health Assessment & Physical Examination* (3rd ed.) by Mary Ellen Zator Estes.

Key Terms

Please define the following terms:

adnexa _____

_____

alopecia _____

_____

amenorrhea _____

_____

anal orifice _____

_____

Bartholin's glands (greater vestibular glands) _____

_____

cervix _____

_____

Chadwick's sign _____

_____

chancre _____

_____

Chandelier's sign _____

_____

clitoris _____

_____

cystocele _____
_____

cystourethrocele _____
_____

dysmenorrhea _____
_____

dyspareunia _____
_____

ectropion (of the cervix) _____
_____

escutcheon _____
_____

eversion (of the cervix) _____
_____

fallopian tubes _____
_____

fornices _____
_____

fourchette _____
_____

fundus _____
_____

hymen _____
_____

isthmus (of the uterus) _____
_____

labia majora _____
_____

labia minora _____
_____

menarche _____
_____

menopause _____
_____

menorrhagia _____
_____

mons pubis _____
_____

Nabothian cysts _____
_____

nulliparous _____

_____

oogenesis _____

_____

ovaries _____

_____

parous _____

_____

perineum _____

_____

rectocele _____

_____

rectouterine pouch _____

_____

Skene's glands (paraurethral glands) _____

_____

spinnbarkeit _____

_____

squamocolumnar junction _____

_____

uterus _____

_____

vagina _____

_____

vaginal introitus _____

_____

vestibule _____

_____

Laboratory Activities

1. Label the following items on the diagram:

   anus
   cervix
   endometrium
   fallopian tube
   myometrium
   ovary
   rectum
   sacrum
   symphysis pubis
   urinary bladder
   uterus
   vagina

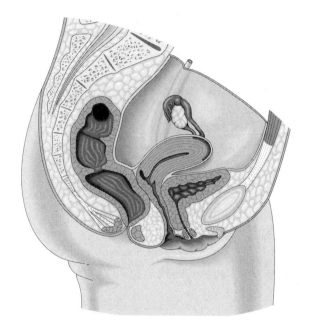

2. What cyclic changes are occurring in the menstrual cycle at the time of ovulation?

   _____
   _____
   _____
   _____

   How does cervical mucus change at ovulation?

   _____
   _____

3. A 20-year-old college student who is sexually active is being seen today for her first gynecological examination. What strategies may help her feel more comfortable before and during the exam?

   _____
   _____
   _____
   _____
   _____
   _____
   _____
   _____

Briefly describe selection and insertion of the speculum.

_____

_____

_____

_____

What characteristics would you note on inspection of the cervix and cervical os?

_____

_____

_____

_____

_____

4. Describe normal findings on palpation of the ovaries and uterus.

_____

_____

_____

_____

_____

5. **ROS (Review of Systems).** Ask your lab partner (or a female patient) the following questions:

Have you had any hx of disease or surgery to the genitalia?

_____

Have you had any hx of vaginal infections, STDs, infertility, CA?

_____

Do you have any pelvic pain, vaginal discharge, or unusual bleeding?

_____

When did you begin menstruating? When was your last menstrual period?

_____

Describe your menstrual flow (frequency, duration, amount).

_____

Do you have any PMS, spotting between menses, or dysmenorrhea?

_____

Have you had been pregnant? Are you pregnant now?

_____

Do you have any symptoms of menopause?

_____

Are you in a satisfactory sexual relationship? Do you have any concerns?

_____

What were the date and results of your last Pap smear?

_____

What is your method of birth control (if any)?

_____

Do you use protection against STDs?

_____

6. **Physical Exam.** *(Equipment: Vaginal speculum, gooseneck lamp, drape, examination table with stirrups, warm water, water-soluble lubricant, gloves.)* Follow the physical assessment guidelines in your text to complete the following information:

Inspection of the External Genitalia

Pubic hair   _____

Skin color and condition

    Mons pubis and vulva   _____

    Clitoris   _____

    Urethral meatus   _____

    Vaginal introitus   _____

    Perineum and anus   _____

Palpation of the External Genitalia

Labia   _____

Urethral meatus and Skene's glands   _____

Vaginal introitus   _____

Perineum   _____

Speculum Examination of the Internal Genitalia

Cervix

    Color   _____

    Position   _____

    Size   _____

    Surface characteristics   _____

    Discharge   _____

    Shape of the cervical os   _____

**Collecting Specimens for Cytological
Smears and Cultures**

Pap smear _____

Endocervical smear _____

Cervical smear _____

Vaginal pool smear _____

Gonococcal culture specimen _____

Saline mount or "wet prep" _____

KOH prep _____

Five percent acetic acid wash _____

Anal culture _____

Inspection of the Vaginal Wall _____

Bimanual Examination

Vagina _____

Cervix _____

Fornices _____

Uterus _____

Adnexa _____

Rectovaginal Examination _____

7. Compare the following abnormal findings for vaginal discharge:

	Color	Odor	Consistency	Cervix
Bacterial vaginosis				
Trichomonas				
Candida				
Gonorrhea				

8. What are the signs of sexual abuse in the female patient?

_____

_____

_____

_____

_____

9. The warning signs of an ectopic pregnancy include:

_____

_____

10. What are the risk factors for cancer of the female genitalia?

Cervical cancer _____

_____

_____

Endometrial cancer _____

_____

_____

Ovarian cancer _____

_____

_____

Vaginal cancer _____

_____

11. Your 52-year-old patient, who is sexually active, had a hysterectomy 1 year ago. What parts of her examination can you omit? What is your recommendation to her for follow-up?

_____

_____

_____

_____

_____

12. You are performing a gynecological exam on a 61-year-old patient. What are your expected findings on examination of her ovaries, uterus, cervix, and vaginal walls?

_____

_____

_____

_____

_____

_____

What normal changes in the aging process may predispose her to each of the following problems?

Vaginal infections _____

Uterine prolapse _____

Dyspareunia _____

Self-Assessment Quiz

1. The Pap smear consists of three specimens, including:

   A. _____

   B. _____

   C. _____

2. True or false?

   ☐ **T** ☐ **F**   The cervical os in a nulliparous woman is a small horizontal slit.

   ☐ **T** ☐ **F**   A Thayer-Martin culture plate is used to detect *Chlamydia trachomatis*.

   ☐ **T** ☐ **F**   The cervix is pale after menopause and blue during pregnancy.

   ☐ **T** ☐ **F**   Swelling or redness around the urethral meatus may indicate a urinary tract infection.

   ☐ **T** ☐ **F**   Bulging on the posterior vaginal wall may indicate a cystocele.

   ☐ **T** ☐ **F**   Strawberry spots on the surface of the cervix may indicate a gonococcal infection.

   ☐ **T** ☐ **F**   The uterus in the nongravid patient is pear shaped.

   ☐ **T** ☐ **F**   Smoking is a risk factor for cervical cancer.

3. In what order would these assessments be performed, and what is each assessing?

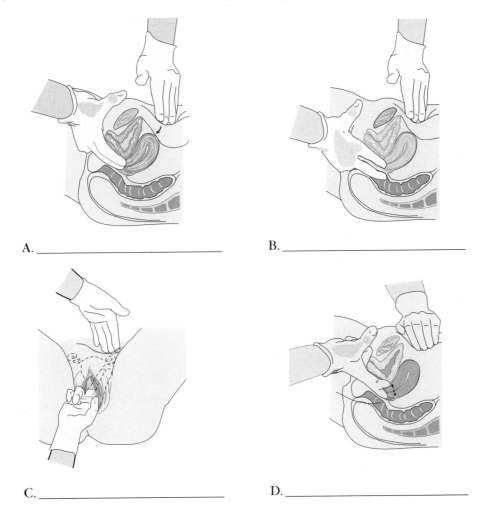

   A. _____   B. _____

   C. _____   D. _____

4. What is wrong with each of these patients?

The first patient is complaining of a discharge that is grayish yellow with a fishy odor; the discharge appears purulent.
She may have _____.

The second patient has a white discharge with the consistency of cottage cheese, but no odor. The vaginal mucosa and vulva look reddened.
She may have _____.

The third patient has several white, dry, cauliflower-like growths on the vulva.
She may have _____.

The fourth patient has small, shallow, red vesicles that fuse together into a large ulcer on the vulva; she is having pain and itching.
She may have _____.

5. The presence of what finding on palpation of the cervix may indicate PID?

_____

Lab Practice for Male Genitalia

Chapter 21

Learning Objectives

1. Identify anatomical structures of the male genitalia.
2. Conduct a review of systems (ROS) for the genitalia.
3. Demonstrate appropriate physical assessment techniques.
4. Differentiate normal and abnormal findings.

Reading Assignment

Before beginning this lab assignment, please read Chapter 21, Male Genitalia, in *Health Assessment & Physical Examination* (3rd ed.) by Mary Ellen Zator Estes.

Key Terms

Please define the following terms:

alopecia _____

_____

bulbourethral glands _____

_____

chancre _____

_____

chancroid _____

_____

condyloma acuminatum _____

_____

cryptorchidism _____

_____

direct inguinal hernia _____

_____

ductus (vas) deferens _____

_____

ejaculatory ducts _____

_____

epididymis_____

_____

epispadias _____

_____

femoral hernia _____

_____

glans penis _____

_____

hydrocele _____

_____

hypospadias _____

_____

indirect inguinal hernia _____

_____

microphallus _____

_____

orchitis _____

_____

paraphimosis _____

_____

penis _____

_____

phimosis _____

_____

prepuce _____

_____

priapism _____

_____

scrotum _____

_____

seminal vesicles _____

_____

smegma _____

_____

spermatic cord _____

_____

spermatocele _____

_____

spermatogenesis _____

_____

testes _____

_____

urethra _____

_____

varicocele _____

_____

Laboratory Activities

1. Label the following items on the drawing:

    bladder
    Cowper's gland
    epididymis
    glans penis
    prostate gland
    rectum
    scrotum
    seminal vesicle
    testis
    urethra
    vas deferens

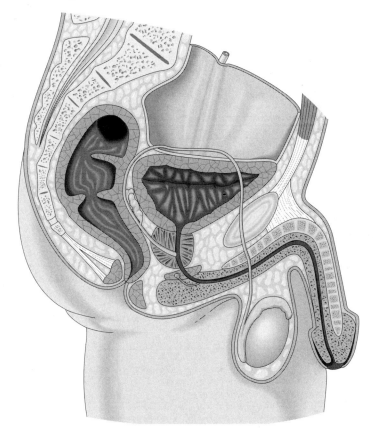

2. What strategies are helpful when examining the male genitalia?

_____

_____

_____

_____

_____

_____

3. Describe normal findings on palpation of the testicles and epididymis.

_____

_____

_____

_____

_____

4. How would you palpate the inguinal area for hernias?

_____

_____

_____

_____

_____

5. How would you teach testicular self-examination (TSE) to your male patient?

_____

_____

_____

_____

_____

6. **ROS (Review of Systems).** Ask a male patient or your lab partner the following questions:

Do you have any hx of disease, surgery, or trauma to the genitalia?

_____

Do you have any urethral discharge, dysuria, or pain?

_____

Do you have any lumps, hernias, or scrotal or prostate enlargement?

_____

Do you have sexual dysfunction?

_____

Do you have a hx of DM, HTN, CAD, CA?

_____

Have you had any exposure to STDs?

_____

Do you use condoms? Do you use supportive devices for sports?

_____

Do you perform TSE? How often?

_____

7. **Physical Exam.** *(Equipment: Stethoscope, penlight, sterile cotton swabs, gloves.)* Follow the physical assessment guidelines in your text to complete the following information:

Inspection

Sexual maturity rating _____

Hair distribution _____

Penis _____

Scrotum _____

Urethral meatus _____

Inguinal area _____

Palpation

Penis _____

Urethral meatus _____

Scrotum _____

Inguinal area _____

Auscultation

Scrotum _____

Advanced Techniques

Prehn's sign (testicular torsion) _____

Transillumination of the scrotum
  (scrotal mass) _____

8. Describe each of these sexually transmitted diseases.

STD	Lesion	Causative Agent
Syphilis		
Genital warts		
Genital herpes simplex		

9. Compare indirect, direct, and femoral hernias.

Hernia	Occurrence	Location	Symptoms
Indirect inguinal			
Direct inguinal			
Femoral			

10. If your patient has a penile discharge, what characteristics should you describe?

_____

_____

_____

11. Compare assessment findings for hydrocele, spermatocele, and varicocele.

_____

_____

_____

12. What changes occur in the male genitalia with aging?

_____

_____

_____

_____

Self-Assessment Quiz

1. Testicular cancer should be suspected if you find _____

_____.

2. Match the following terms and descriptions:

_____ Spontaneous descent after age 1 is unusual

_____ Can be caused by mumps, varicella

_____ May accompany CHF and renal failure

_____ Feels like a "bag of worms" to palpation

_____ Usually caused by bacterial pathogens from urethra

_____ A surgical emergency

_____ Nodular, associated with painless swelling

A. testicular torsion

B. testicular tumor

C. epididymitis

D. orchitis

E. cryptorchidism

F. scrotal edema

G. varicocele

3. Auscultation of a scrotal mass may be performed to determine _____.

4. True or false?

    ☐ **T** ☐ **F** Hypospadias occurs when the urethral meatus opens dorsally on the glans.
    ☐ **T** ☐ **F** A chancroid is the lesion of primary syphilis and is highly infectious.
    ☐ **T** ☐ **F** A male patient may be unaware of an HPV infection for months or years.
    ☐ **T** ☐ **F** Small (1 cm) mobile lymph nodes in the inguinal area are normal.
    ☐ **T** ☐ **F** Oval swelling at the symphysis pubis is noted with a femoral hernia.

5. Warning signs of STDs in the male patient include:

_____
_____
_____
_____
_____

6. Name the condition shown in each of the following.

A. _____   B. _____   C. _____

Lab Practice for Anus, Rectum, and Prostate

Learning Objectives

1. Locate anatomical structures of the rectum and prostate gland.
2. Conduct a review of systems (ROS) for the rectum and prostate gland.
3. Demonstrate appropriate physical assessment techniques.
4. Differentiate normal and abnormal findings.

Reading Assignment

Before beginning this lab assignment, please read Chapter 22, Anus, Rectum, and Prostate, in *Health Assessment & Physical Examination* (3rd ed.) by Mary Ellen Zator Estes.

Key Terms

Please define the following terms:

anal canal _____

_____

anal columns _____

_____

anal fissure _____

_____

anal incontinence _____

_____

anal sinuses _____

_____

anal valves _____

_____

anoderm _____

_____

anorectal abscess _____

_____

anorectal fistula _____

_____

anorectum _____

_____

defecation _____
_____

hemorrhoids _____
_____

melena _____
_____

prostate _____
_____

rectal prolapse _____
_____

rectum _____
_____

steatorrhea _____
_____

Laboratory Activities

1. Label the following anatomical structures:

   anal canal
   anorectal junction
   bladder
   bulbourethral (Cowper's) gland
   prostate gland
   rectum

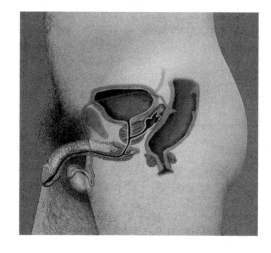

2. What measures can increase your patient's comfort with the anal, rectal, and prostate exam?

_____
_____
_____
_____
_____

3. **ROS (Review of Systems).** Ask a male patient or your lab partner the following questions:

Do you have a hx of bowel or prostate disease or surgery?

_____

Do you have a hx of STDs or rectal trauma?

_____

Do you have hemorrhoids, itching, masses, or polyps?

_____

Do you experience constipation, diarrhea, or incontinence?

_____

Have you had any changes in your stool?

_____

Do you have any pain or discharge of blood from the rectum?

_____

Have you had any change in your weight or appetite?

_____

Have you ever had a colonoscopy or flexible sigmoidoscopy?

_____

4. **Physical Exam.** *(Equipment: Water-soluble lubricant, hemoccult cards, lamp, gloves.)* Follow the physical assessment guidelines in your text to complete the following information:

Inspection

Perineum and sacrococcygeal area _____

Anal mucosa _____

_____

Palpation

Anus and rectum _____

_____

Prostate _____

_____

5. What are some common causes of rectal bleeding?

   _____

   _____

   _____

   _____

   _____

6. Risk factors for colorectal cancer include:

   _____

   _____

   _____

   _____

   _____

7. What assessment findings may lead you to suspect rectal abuse?

   _____

   _____

   _____

8. What are the causes of each of the following problems in the aging population?

   Urinary obstruction _____

   Fecal incontinence _____

   Rectal prolapse _____

   Constipation _____

   UTIs _____

9. What signs and symptoms are associated with acute bacterial prostatitis?

   _____

   _____

   _____

   Why is rectal examination avoided?

   _____

   _____

Self-Assessment Quiz

1. What are the risk factors for prostate cancer?

   A. _____

   B. _____

   C. _____

   D. _____

   E. _____

2. Match the terms with the correct description:

_____ Related to aging and the presence of testosterone	A. hemorrhoids
_____ Results from upper gastrointestinal bleeding	B. anal fissure
_____ Noted in malabsorption syndrome	C. rectal prolapse
_____ May result from heavy lifting, childbirth, or straining	D. melena
_____ Firm, hard, or indurated nodules may be noted	E. steatorrhea
_____ Appears as pinkish-red "doughnut" at anal orifice	F. prostate cancer
_____ Often seen in Crohn's disease	G. benign prostatic hypertrophy

3. True or false?

   ☐ T ☐ F Rectal polyps occur frequently in the general population of the United States.

   ☐ T ☐ F Prostatic abscesses are associated with diabetes mellitus.

   ☐ T ☐ F There is a strong association between HSV-2 and anal carcinoma.

   ☐ T ☐ F Bacterial prostatitis is usually caused by *Escherichia coli.*

   ☐ T ☐ F Black, tarry stool indicates rectal bleeding.

   ☐ T ☐ F Mucoid or creamy exudate from the rectum is a finding in gonococcal proctitis.

4. Name the assessment technique that is demonstrated in each of these pictures.

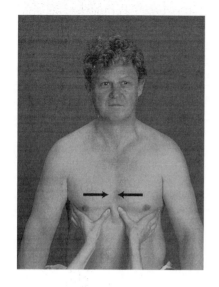

A. _____

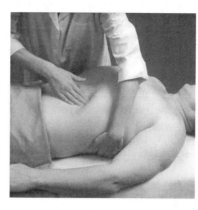

B. _____

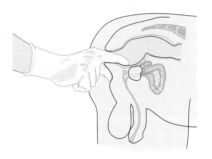

C. _____

D. _____

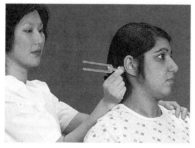

E. _____

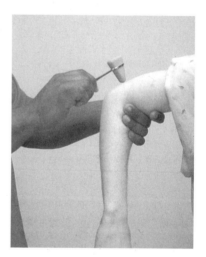

F. _____

Lab Practice for Pregnant Patient

Learning Objectives

1. Describe alterations in the physiological system of the pregnant patient.
2. Collect information for an obstetrical history.
3. Demonstrate a physical assessment of the pregnant patient.
4. Demonstrate Leopold's maneuver and fundal height measurement.

Reading Assignment

Before beginning this lab assignment, please read Chapter 23, Pregnant Patient, in *Health Assessment & Physical Examination* (3rd ed.) by Mary Ellen Zator Estes.

Key Terms

Please define the following terms:

Braxton Hicks contractions _____

_____

chloasma _____

_____

colostrum _____

_____

diastasis recti_____

_____

eclampsia_____

_____

ectopic pregnancy _____

_____

ectropion (or eversion, of the cervix) _____

_____

fetoscope_____

_____

friability _____

_____

glycosuria _____

_____

HELLP syndrome _____

hyperemesis gravidarum _____

lightening _____

linea nigra _____

macrosomia _____

melasma _____

nocturia _____

proteinuria _____

prurigo _____

ptyalism _____

quickening _____

striae gravidarum _____

Laboratory Activities

1. Write out Naegele's rule for determining the delivery date based on the LMP.

   _____
   _____
   _____
   _____

   Using Naegele's rule, determine the EDD (or EDC) for each of these patients.

	LMP	EDD/EDC
Patient A	February 3	
Patient B	June 15	
Patient C	December 30	

2. What does each of the following sets of abbreviations mean?

G: 4   T: 2   P: 2   A: 2   LC: 2 _____

_____

G: 2   T: 0   P: 0   A: 2   LC: 0 _____

_____

G: 3   T: 1   P: 1   A: 0   LC: 1 _____

_____

3. What are some of the normal and abnormal findings in the following physiological systems for the pregnant patient?

System	Normal Changes	Abnormal Findings
Skin and hair		
Head and neck		
Eyes, ears, nose, mouth, and throat		
Breasts		
Thorax and lungs		
Heart and peripheral vasculature		
Abdomen		
Urinary system		
Musculoskeletal system		
Neurological system		

System	Normal Changes	Abnormal Findings
Hematological system		
Endocrine system		
Female genitalia		

4. Your patient is here today for an initial visit with her third pregnancy. She tells you her LMP was exactly 10 weeks ago. What is her EDD? _____ What presumptive signs of pregnancy might she be experiencing?

_____

_____

_____

5. What are the danger signs of pregnancy?

A. _____

B. _____

C. _____

D. _____

E. _____

F. _____

G. _____

H. _____

I. _____

Describe cervical changes that have occurred.

_____

_____

_____

What laboratory tests might be performed on this visit?

_____

_____

_____

_____

One of her return prenatal visits will be at 26–28 weeks. Which tests will be added or repeated at that time?

_____

_____

_____

At a follow-up appointment, your patient complains of increased vaginal discharge and occasional leg cramps. What recommendations could you give?

_____

_____

_____

Your patient is now identified as having a high-risk pregnancy at 34 weeks. What tests for fetal well-being could be performed?

_____

_____

_____

6. **Obstetric History.** Ask a pregnant patient or your lab partner the following questions regarding her present and previous obstetric history:

Present Obstetric History

When was the LMP?

_____

What is the hx since LMP (fever, rashes, disease or toxic exposure, abnormal bleeding, nausea and vomiting)?

_____

Are there signs and symptoms of pregnancy?

_____

Have you used fertility drugs?

_____

Calculate the EDD/EDC.

_____

What are your or your family's genetic predispositions?

_____

Past Obstetric History

*Gravidity, full-term births, preterm births, abortions,
ectopic pregnancies, number of living children*

G _____ P _____ T _____ P _____ A _____ E _____ LC _____

Date of delivery				
Vaginal/cesarian				
Length of labor				
Meds/anesthesia				
Infant sex/weight				
Infant Apgar scores				
Feeding (breast or bottle)				

Any complications: Pregnancy, labor and delivery, postpartum

_____

_____

_____

_____

_____

_____

Any hx of uterine or abdominal injury or surgery?

_____

Have you been exposed to communicable disease?
Have you been immunized for rubella?

_____

Are you on any medications (Rx or OTC)?

_____

Do you use any alcohol, tobacco, or drugs?

_____

7. **Physical Exam.** *(Equipment: Stethoscope, Doppler/fetoscope, centimeter tape measure, watch with a second hand.)* Follow the physical assessment guidelines in your text to complete the following information:

Fundal Height _____

Fetal Heart Rate _____

Leopold's Maneuver
    First maneuver   _____
    Second maneuver   _____
    Third maneuver   _____
    Fourth maneuver   _____

8. A uterine size that is larger than expected (according to LMP) may indicate:

_____
_____
_____

A uterine size smaller than expected may indicate:

_____
_____
_____

9. How is ultrasound used during a pregnancy?

_____
_____
_____

10. Your pregnant patient with diabetes mellitus is at increased risk for what complications?

_____
_____
_____
_____

11. How would you determine whether your patient has PIH or chronic hypertension?

_____
_____
_____
_____

12. Identify signs that may indicate abuse in the pregnant patient.

_____
_____

Self-Assessment Quiz

1. Which of these lab results of the pregnant patient need follow-up?

   mild glycosuria   HCT 34%

   HGB 14%   glucose screen 150 mg/dl post glucola

   Rh negative   trace of proteinuria

2. What do you know about these important first events?

   A. Quickening is typically first noted by the pregnant woman at _____ weeks.

   B. If a pregnancy is "at-risk," fetal kick counts should first be done at _____ weeks.

   C. A Doppler can first be used to hear FHTs at _____ weeks.

   D. The first Leopold's maneuver determines _____.

   E. A woman pregnant for the first time will be a "G: _____ T: _____ P: _____."

   F. If a pregnant patient has edema, hypertension, and proteinuria, the caregiver should first suspect _____.

3. Please match the following terms and definitions for the pregnant patient.

   _____ Most common cause of proteinuria

   _____ Cervical softening

   _____ Occurs with descent of presenting fetal part into the pelvis

   _____ Softening of the uterine isthmus

   _____ Most common cause of seizures

   _____ Bluish hue to the cervix

   _____ Blotchy, irregular pigmentation

   _____ Separation of abdominal muscle

   _____ One of the most common causes of abdominal pain

   A. chloasma

   B. eclampsia

   C. Chadwick's sign

   D. PIH

   E. Goodell's sign

   F. abruptio placenta

   G. diastasis recti

   H. lightening

   I. Hegar's sign

4. Label the following as normal or abnormal.

   _____ A fundus measured at 2 cm above the umbilicus at 22 weeks

   _____ Nitrates in the urine

   _____ FHTs showing tachycardia at 26 weeks

   _____ A drop in fundal height at 40 weeks

   _____ Hyperreflexia

   _____ A white, milky cervical discharge

5. The following drawings show a nurse palpating the abdomen to determine positioning of the fetus. What is the name of this technique?

_____

Identify the proper sequence:

 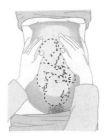  

A. _____   B. _____   C. _____   D. _____

6. Which of the following provide positive signs of pregnancy?

quickening   fetal outline

fetal heartbeats   Braxton Hicks contractions

ballottement   ultrasound

positive pregnancy test   amenorrhea

Lab Practice for Pediatric Patient

Learning Objectives

1. Compare physiological differences between pediatric and adult patients.
2. Conduct a review of systems (ROS) for the pediatric patient.
3. Demonstrate appropriate physical assessment techniques.
4. Differentiate normal and abnormal findings.
5. Describe strategies that facilitate assessment on an infant or child.

Reading Assignment

Before beginning this lab assignment, please read Chapter 24, Pediatric Patient, in *Health Assessment & Physical Examination* (3rd ed.) by Mary Ellen Zator Estes.

Key Terms

Please define the following terms:

acrocyanosis _____

_____

anencephaly _____

_____

Apgar score _____

_____

attention deficit hyperactivity disorder _____

_____

Brushfield's spots _____

_____

caput succedaneum _____

_____

cephalhematoma _____

_____

clubfoot _____

_____

cradle cap _____

_____

craniosynostosis _____

_____

craniotabes _____

_____

cryptorchidism _____

_____

developmental dysplasia of the hip _____

_____

diaphragmatic hernia _____

_____

Epstein's pearls _____

_____

harlequin color change _____

_____

hydrocephalus _____

_____

intussusception _____

_____

lanugo _____

_____

meconium _____

_____

metatarsus varus _____

_____

microcephaly _____

_____

microphallus _____

_____

milia _____

_____

molding _____

_____

Mongolian spots _____

_____

physiological weight loss _____

_____

stork bites _____

_____

talipes equinovarus _____

_____

telangiectatic nevi _____

_____

vernix caseosa _____

_____

Laboratory Activities

1. List the structural and physiological variations in each of the following systems in a child:

System	Variations
Vital signs	
Skin, hair	
Head	
Eyes, ears	
Nose, mouth, throat	
Breasts	
Thorax, lungs	
Heart, peripheral vasculature	
Abdomen	
Musculoskeletal	
Neurological	
Female genitalia	
Male genitalia	

2. What is the purpose of the Denver II tool?

How is the Denver II administered?

_____

_____

_____

_____

_____

According to the Denver II tool, at what age are 90% of children able to:

Drink from a cup?_____

Copy a circle? _____

Imitate speech sounds? _____

Roll over?_____

3. How do you perform Apgar scoring of a newborn?

_____

_____

_____

_____

_____

What are possible causes of a low Apgar score?

_____

_____

_____

4. Until what age should each of the following be assessed?

Ortolani's maneuver_____

Head circumference_____

Chest circumference _____

5. What general approaches to the pediatric assessment may help your patient be more comfortable and cooperative?

For an infant?

_____

_____

_____

_____

_____

For a toddler or preschooler?

_____

_____

_____

_____

_____

For an older child?

_____

_____

_____

_____

_____

6. Describe the method for eliciting each of the following reflexes in the newborn.

Reflex	Method	Normal Response
Rooting		
Sucking		
Palmar grasp		
Tonic neck		
Stepping		
Plantar grasp		
Babinski's		
Moro		
Placing		
Galant		
Landau		

7. Describe three methods for holding an infant or a child for an otoscopic examination.

   A. _____

   B. _____

   C. _____

8. **Health History.** Ask a pediatric patient or caregiver the following questions *(note the source and reliability of the information):*

   When did the mother's prenatal care begin?

   _____

   Was it a full-term or a preterm birth?

   _____

   Were there any complications of pregnancy, labor, or birth?

   _____

   Is there any significant family hx, including SIDS, congenital defects, or mental retardation?

   _____

   Does the child have frequent injuries or accidents?

   _____

   Were there any hospitalizations or ER visits?

   _____

   Has the child had any exposure to measles, mumps, rubella, pertussis, or chickenpox?

   _____

   Is the child current on immunizations?

   _____

   Are there any unusual physical complaints?

   _____

   Are there frequent episodes of illness?

   _____

   Have there been any changes in usual sleep patterns?

   _____

   Are there any concerns or problems with current eating habits?

   _____

   Has any regression to outgrown behaviors been noted?

   _____

What activities does the child enjoy?

_____

How does the child express anger or cope with stress?

_____

Is the child in daycare?

_____

Have measures been taken to childproof the home?

_____

9. **Physical Exam.** *(Equipment: Scale, appropriate-sized blood pressure cuff, Snellen E chart, Tumbling E chart, Allen cards, ophthalmoscope, otoscope speculum (2.5 or 4.0 mm), pediatric stethoscope, growth chart, small bell, brightly colored object, Denver II materials, clean gloves, disposable centimeter tape measure.)* Follow the physical assessment guidelines in your text to complete the following information:

Developmental Assessment
Denver II (birth–6 years)   _____

_____
_____
_____

Physical Growth
Weight   _____
Length/height   _____
Head circumference   _____
Chest circumference   _____

Physical Assessment
Apgar scoring (birth)   _____
Head
   Inspection
      Head control   _____
   Palpation
      Anterior fontanel   _____
      Posterior fontanel   _____
      Suture lines   _____
      Surface characteristics   _____
Eyes
   Vision screening
      Allen test (2–4 years)   _____

Musculoskeletal system

  Inspection

    Tibiofemoral bones   _____

  Palpation

    Feet (metatarsus varus)   _____

    Hip and femur (Ortolani

      maneuver) (birth–8 months)   _____

Neurological system

  Rooting   _____

  Sucking   _____

  Palmar grasp   _____

  Tonic neck   _____

  Stepping   _____

  Plantar grasp   _____

  Babinski   _____

  Moro (startle)   _____

  Galant   _____

  Placing   _____

  Landau   _____

Advanced Techniques

Transillumination of the skull

  (hydrocephalus, anencephaly)   _____

Assessing for coarctation of the aorta   _____

10. How can you assess the cranial nerves on a toddler or a preschooler?

_____

_____

_____

_____

_____

11. Briefly describe a holosystolic murmur and diastolic murmurs.

_____

_____

_____

_____

_____

_____

12. What behavioral changes might be noted in an infant with congestive heart failure?

_____

_____

_____

What respiratory signs might be exhibited?

_____

_____

_____

_____

13. What are some safety tips to include in your teaching for the parents of an infant?

_____

_____

_____

_____

_____

14. List possible signs that might be noted on the skin of a child who is physically abused.

_____

_____

_____

_____

Identify signs that might indicate sexual abuse in a child.

_____

_____

_____

_____

15. Which immunizations will you administer to your 1-year-old patient?

_____

_____

_____

Which immunizations will the child receive before starting school?

_____

_____

16. You are examining an infant who is LGA and was in a breech presentation. What findings might indicate DDH?

_____

_____

_____

Self-Assessment Quiz

1. According to averages, a baby who weighs 8 pounds and is 20 inches in length at birth would be expected:

   At 6 months: to weigh _____, with a length of _____

   At 1 year: to weigh _____, with a length of _____

2. Match the following findings on the newborn:

_____ Changes from pale to ruddy color at midline	A. lanugo
_____ Premature ossification of suture lines	B. cephalhematoma
_____ Seborrheic dermatitis	C. acrocyanosis
_____ Localized, subcutaneous swelling over a cranial bone	D. Mongolian spots
_____ Small white flecks around perimeter of the iris	E. stork bites
_____ Most prominent on upper arms, shoulders, back	F. cradle cap
_____ From pressure over occipitoparietal region during prolonged delivery	G. harlequin color change
_____ Telangiectatic nevi	H. craniosynostosis
_____ Bluish purple color of the hands and feet	I. caput succedaneum
_____ Deep-blue pigmentation over lumbar and sacral areas	J. Brushfield's spots

3. According to the rule of thumb for determining normal blood pressure values, what would be the expected normal blood pressure for a 2-year-old child? _____

4. True or false?

   ☐ T ☐ F   Rooting and sucking reflexes are gone by the age of 10 months.
   ☐ T ☐ F   Palpable pulsation in the anterior fontanel is normal.
   ☐ T ☐ F   The Babinski reflex usually disappears at the age of 2 years.
   ☐ T ☐ F   Chest circumference is greater than head circumference at 1 year.
   ☐ T ☐ F   Infants lose up to 10% of their birth weight by 3 days of age.
   ☐ T ☐ F   Fifty percent of all children develop an innocent murmur.
   ☐ T ☐ F   Visual acuity of the newborn is 20/100.
   ☐ T ☐ F   Tonsils graded 2+ at the age of 10 are normal.
   ☐ T ☐ F   Genu varum (bow leg) is common from age 2 to 4 years.
   ☐ T ☐ F   Bronchovesicular breath sounds in the peripheral lung fields at the age of 5 are normal.

5. What are the Apgar scores for each of the following newborn infants?

	Infant A	Infant B	Infant C	Infant D
Heart rate	102	140	90	126
Respiratory rate	Slow, irregular	Crying vigorously	Slow, irregular	Crying
Muscle tone	Extremities slightly flexed	Active movement	Flaccid	Slight flexion
Reflex irritability	Grimaces	Crying	No response	Crying
Color	Body pink, extremities blue	Body pink, hands and feet blue	Cyanotic	Body pink, extremities blue

Apgar score

6. "When will my baby ..."

   A. cry real tears? _____
   B. shiver when she's cold? _____
   C. double his birth weight? _____
   D. get her first tooth? _____
   E. start his DTP shots? _____
   F. really smile at me? _____

Lab Practice for the Complete Health History and Physical Examination

Chapter 25

Learning Objectives

1. Review legal considerations for nursing practice.
2. Identify characteristics of a successful assessment.
3. Demonstrate an integrated physical examination.

Reading Assignment

Before beginning this lab assignment, please read Chapter 25, The Complete Health History and Physical Examination, in *Health Assessment & Physical Examination* (3rd ed.) by Mary Ellen Zator Estes.

Laboratory Activities

1. What are some of the legal guidelines to follow to help protect you and your patient?

    _____
    _____
    _____
    _____
    _____
    _____

2. You are preparing to perform a physical examination on a 57-year-old female patient who appears to be quite anxious. How can you adjust the physical surroundings and your approach to help her feel more at ease?

    _____
    _____
    _____
    _____
    _____

3. How can you obtain information for the mental status assessment?

_____

_____

_____

_____

_____

4. How do you incorporate examination of the skin into your health assessment?

_____

_____

_____

5. **Physical Exam.** *(Equipment: All items listed in previous chapters.)* Complete the health history and review of systems as noted in the text. Then follow the physical assessment guidelines in your text to conduct an integrated physical assessment. Remember to give simple, easy-to-follow instructions as needed.

General Survey   _____

Neurological System   _____

Measurements   _____

Skin   _____

Head and Face   _____

Eyes   _____

Ears   _____

Nose and Sinuses   _____

Mouth and Throat   _____

Neck   _____

Upper Extremities   _____

**Back, Posterior and
  Lateral Thoraxes**   _____

Anterior Thorax   _____

Heart   _____

Breasts   _____

Jugular Veins   _____

Abdomen _____

Inguinal Area _____

Lower Extremities _____

Musculoskeletal System _____

Female Genitalia, Anus,
  and Rectum _____

Male Genitalia, Anus, Rectum,
  Prostate _____

Problem List

Onset date	Problem number	Active problem	Inactive problem

6. What strategies can make an elderly patient more comfortable during an exam?

_____

_____

_____

_____

7. How would you proceed with a patient who:

    A. seems hesitant about a having a particular part of the assessment performed?

    _____

    _____

    _____

    B. refuses to answer certain questions?

    _____

    _____

    _____

8. Which reflexes would be assessed in the comatose patient?

    _____

    _____

    _____

9. How can you show sensitivity when communicating bad news to a patient?

_____

_____

_____

_____

10. What conditions would contraindicate your patient's ability to do sports?

_____

_____

_____

Self-Assessment Quiz

1. True or false?

☐ **T** ☐ **F**   Being truthful with a patient demonstrates the ethical principle of justice.

☐ **T** ☐ **F**   Incorporate assessment of any assistive devices into the physical examination.

☐ **T** ☐ **F**   Mental status is assessed before having the patient undress.

☐ **T** ☐ **F**   Allow time after the physical exam to teach the patient self-assessment techniques.

☐ **T** ☐ **F**   The two areas of greatest emphasis in athletic evaluation are cardiovascular and respiratory.

2. Put the following assessments in the correct sequence for an integrated head-to-toe exam.

A. deep tendon reflexes

B. posterior thorax

C. anterior thorax

D. jugular veins

E. abdomen

F. genitalia

G. breasts

H. neck

I. ears

3. What is the actual medical term for each of the following?

   Eardrum _____

   Adam's apple _____

   Hammer (bone in middle ear) _____

   Black and blue marks _____

   Shoulder blades _____

   Swollen glands _____

   Womb _____

   Breastbone _____

   Ear wax _____

   Soft spot _____

   Knee cap _____

   Taste buds _____

4. Your entire plan of care for a patient is based on _____.

Answers to Self-Assessment Quizzes

Chapter 1: Critical Thinking and the Nursing Process

1. assessment, nursing diagnosis, outcome identification, planning, implementation, evaluation

2. E   O
   O, I   I
   A   E
   P   D
   A, D

3. F   T   F   F   T   T

4. B and D

5. nursing care plan

Chapter 2: The Patient Interview

1. Active listening

2. leading questions, interrupting the patient, talkativeness, multiple questions, using medical jargon

3. F   T   T   T   F

4. exploring, reflecting, focusing, encouraging comparisons, normalizing

5. defining appropriate boundaries, sharing personal reactions, refocusing the patient

Chapter 3: The Complete Health History Including Documentation

1. complete, episodic, interval or follow-up, emergency

2. E, G, I, G, A, B, D, F, C, H, I

3. F   T   T   F   F   T   F   F   F

4. Not mentioned by the patient: radiation, quantity, associated manifestations

5.

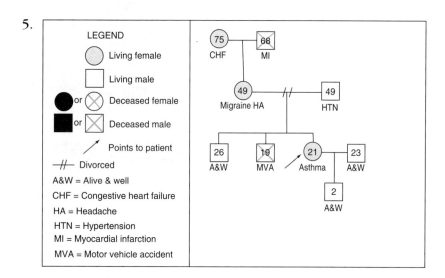

6. "In the past year, have you been hit, kicked, punched, or hurt in other ways by someone close to you?"

Chapter 4: Developmental Assessment

1. Erikson's epigenetic theory of personality

2. young adult   infancy   school-age children
   late middle adulthood   toddler   adolescence
   preschooler

3. F   T   F   T   T   F

4. D, F, E, C, A, B

5. life review

Chapter 5: Cultural Assessment

1. Culture

2. T   F   T   F   F   T   T

3. acculturation

4. H, F, G, A, E, D, B, C

5. culture shock

Chapter 6: Spiritual Assessment

1. spiritual distress, readiness for enhanced spiritual well-being

2. F   T   F   T   F   T

3. A. spirituality   C. Dogma   E. spiritual distress
   B. Reincarnation   D. Animism

4. platitude
   cliché

5. N, H   J, P   I   B
   N   B   R
   H   J   I

Chapter 7: Nutritional Assessment

1. health promotion
informing at-risk individuals of physical, cognitive, psychological, and social changes that occur
explaining individuals' nutritional needs

2. G, E, G and H, B, A, D, F, C, H, C, E

3. adequate nutrients within calorie needs; weight management; physical activity; food groups to encourage; fats; carbohydrates; sodium and potassium; alcoholic beverages

4. Patient C (due to possible insufficient calories and fluids for supporting breastfeeding)

5. A. 50–60   B. 120   C. 10–20   D. 90

6. diabetes mellitus, coronary artery disease

Chapter 8: Physical Assessment Techniques

1. A. direct or immediate   B. indirect or mediate   C. direct fist   D. indirect fist
For the kidney—Indirect fist percussion

2. F   F   T   T   F   T   F

3. A. dorsal recumbent   B. lithotomy   C. Sims'   D. semi-Fowler's

4. E, D, A, C, B, A, C

5. validation of complaints   monitoring of current health problems
screening of general well-being   formulating diagnoses and treatments

Chapter 9: General Survey, Vital Signs, and Pain

1. G, I   B   C   J
   D, I, J   D   F   H
   J   C   H

2. A. temporal   D. brachial   G. popliteal
   B. carotid   E. radial   H. posterior tibial
   C. apical   F. femoral   I. dorsalis pedis

3. ineffective pumping, decreased circulating volume, changes in characteristics of blood vessels, diurnal variation

4. T   F   F   T   T   F   F

5. A. 98.6   B. 100.4   C. 36.4   D. 38.3

6. Wong-Baker FACES Pain Rating Scale, the Oucher Pain Assessment Tool

Chapter 10: Skin, Hair, and Nails

1. moisture, temperature, tenderness, texture, turgor, edema, color, bleeding, ecchymosis, vascularity, lesions

2. C (180°)

3.
tumor P	papule P	cyst P
keloid S	fissure S	lichenification S
erosion S	ulcer S	pustule P
vesicle P	crust S	scar S

4. F, D, B, H, A, C, E, G

5. A. annulae   B. linear   C. confluent   D. zosteriform

6. A. asymmetrical   B. borders   C. color   D. diameter   E. elevation

Chapter 11: Head, Neck, and Regional Lymphatics

1. Refer to your text, Figure 11-3, Anterior and Posterior Cervical Triangles
   A. anterior cervical lymph nodes, trachea, thyroid   B. posterior cervical lymph nodes

2. C, A, E, B, F, D

3. A. sternocleidomastoid muscle   F. left lobe of thyroid
   B. hyoid bone   G. trachea
   C. thyroid cartilage   H. sternum
   D. cricoid cartilage   I. clavicle
   E. isthmus of thyroid   J. right lobe of thyroid

4. age 5–50, female, family history of migraines, allergies, Raynaud's, history of motion sickness, increased stress, estrogen, caffeine, tyramine/MSG/nitrate consumption, sleep disorders

5.
normal	abnormal
abnormal	abnormal
normal	

Chapter 12: Eyes

1. fovea centralis

2. A. vein   B. artery   C. physiologic cup   D. disc margin   E. optic disc
   F. fovea centralis   G. macula;
   left eye

3. E, F, H, G, I, C, A, B, D

4. F   F   T   T   F   F

5. A. hordeolum   B. myopia

6. Corrected vision that is 20/200 (or worse), or peripheral vision that is less than 20°.

Chapter 13: Ears, Nose, Mouth, and Throat

1. Pearly gray with clearly defined landmarks; distinct cone-shaped light reflex extending from the umbo at 5:00 position in the right ear and 7:00 position in the left; no bulging or retracting, no fluid, no perforations

2. lateralization to the left ear
   bone conduction equal to or greater than air conduction in left ear

3. normal   normal   normal
   abnormal   normal

4. transillumination

5. oral hairy leukoplakia, torus mandibularis, scrotal tongue, torus palatinus, Fordyce's spots, hemangioma

6. along the lateral surfaces of the tongue

Chapter 14: Breasts and Regional Nodes

1. location, size, shape, number, consistency, definition, mobility, tenderness, erythema, dimpling or retraction, lymphadenopathy

2. A, C, F, G

3. All are risk factors

4. T   T   T   F   F

5. A. palpation of infraclavicular nodes
   B. bimanual palpation
   C. palpation of axillary nodes

Chapter 15: Thorax and Lungs

1. A. vesicular
   B. increased carbon dioxide level, decreased oxygen level, increased blood pH level
   C. long-standing hypoxia
   D. crepitus

2. E, G, F, B, D, C, A

3. A. tachypnea   B. Cheyne-Stokes   C. Kussmaul's   D. Biot's

4. Patient A: normal   Patient D: abnormal
   Patient B: abnormal   Patient E: normal
   Patient C: normal

5. C   A   A, D
   B, D   A   A
   B, D   C

6. smoking tobacco, secondhand tobacco smoke exposure, smokers with COPD, hereditary predisposition, occupational or environmental exposure to carcinogens (asbestos, radon, heavy metals)

Chapter 16: Heart and Peripheral Vasculature

1. superior/inferior vena cava → right atrium → tricuspid valve → right ventricle → pulmonic valve → (pulmonary artery, lungs, pulmonary vein) → left atrium → mitral valve → left ventricle → aortic valve → aorta

2. F   T   T   F   T   F   F   T   T

3. C, E, F, B, D, A

4. age, gender, race, family hx, hypertension, hyperlipidemia, use of tobacco, diabetes, sedentary lifestyle, diet, stress, obesity (risk factors that are fixed: age, gender, race, family hx)

5. D, G, F, B, A, C, E

Chapter 17: Abdomen

1. diaphragm, symphysis pubis

2. A   C
   C   All
   B   D
   A   C and D
   A   C

3. bell   bell
   diaphragm   diaphragm
   bell   bell
   diaphragm   both

4. normal   normal   normal
      normal   abnormal   abnormal
      abnormal   normal

5. fat, fluid (ascites), flatus, feces, fetus, fatal growth (malignancy), fibroid tumor

6. A. referred pain   E. signs of discomfort or pain
   B. last   F. gallbladder
   C. cough   G. pain
   D. involuntary muscle guarding   H. appendicitis

Chapter 18: Musculoskeletal System

1. C, G, H, F, D, E, A, I, B

2. 4, 5

3. F   F   F   T   T   F

4. G, C, F, A, H, E, B, D

5. All are true.

6. A. scoliosis   B. lordosis   C. list   D. kyphosis

7. the straight leg raising test (Lasègue's test) or Milgram test

Chapter 19: Mental Status and Neurological Techniques

1. G   E
    C   H
    B   D
    A, F   A

2. A. brachioradialis   B. Achilles   C. patellar

3. F   T   T   F   F   T

4. XI, IX and X, VII, II, VIII, III

5. nuchal rigidity, Kernig's sign, Brudzinski's sign

Chapter 20: Female Genitalia

1. endocervical smear, cervical smear, vaginal pool smear

2. F   F   T   F   F   F   T   T

3. A. second, uterus   C. third, adnexa
   B. fourth, rectovaginal area   D. first, cervical mobility

4. trichomoniasis
candidiasis
venereal warts (human papillomavirus—HPV)
genital herpes (herpes simplex)

5. positive Chandelier's sign

Chapter 21: Male Genitalia

1. a hard, fixed nodule on the testicle

2. E, D, F, G, C, A, B

3. the presence of bowel sounds (indirect inguinal hernia)

4. F   F   T   T   F

5. bloody or purulent penile discharge, scrotal and/or testicular pain, burning and/or pain on urination, penile lesion

6. A. cryptorchidism   B. epididymitis   C. testicular torsion

Chapter 22: Anus, Rectum, and Prostate

1. A. over age 50   D. high intake of fats, oil, and sugar
B. family history of prostate cancer   E. high levels of serum testosterone
C. Black American

2. G (and F), D, E, A, F, C, B

3. T   T   F   T   F   T

4. A. thoracic expansion   D. rectovaginal exam
B. palpation of spleen   E. Rinne test (bone conduction)
C. palpation of bulbourethral gland   F. assessment of triceps reflex

Chapter 23: Pregnant Patient

1. HCT 34%
glucose screen 150 mg/dl post glucola

2. A. 18-20   D. Which fetal part presents at the fundus
B. 28   E. G:1   T:0   P:0
C. 12   F. PIH

3. D, E, H, I, B, C, A, G, F

4. normal   normal
   abnormal   abnormal
   normal   normal

5. Leopold's maneuver
   - A. Second
   - B. First
   - C. Fourth
   - D. Third

6. fetal heartbeats, fetal outline, ultrasound

Chapter 24: Pediatric Patient

1. 16 pounds, 26 inches
   24 pounds, 29 inches

2. G, H, F, B, J, A, I, E, C, D

3. 84/56

4. T   T   F   F   T   T   F   T   F   T

5. 6, 9, 2, 8

6.
   - A. 2–3 months
   - B. 6 months
   - C. 6 months
   - D. 5–7 months
   - E. 2 months
   - F. 2 months

Chapter 25: The Complete Health History and Physical Examination

1. F   T   T   F   F

2.
   - I. ears
   - H. neck
   - B. posterior thorax
   - C. anterior thorax
   - G. breasts
   - D. jugular veins
   - E. abdomen
   - A. deep tendon reflexes
   - F. genitalia

3. tympanic membrane
   thyroid cartilage
   malleus
   ecchymosis
   scapulae
   lymphadenopathy (enlarged lymph nodes)

   uterus
   sternum
   cerumen
   (anterior) fontanel
   patella
   papillae

4. patient assessment

Appendix B

Abbreviations

ADL	activities of daily living		GI	gastrointestinal
AIDS	acquired immunodeficiency syndrome		HCT	hematocrit
AP	anteroposterior		HEADSS	Home, Education, Activities, Drugs, Sex, and Suicide Adolescent Risk Profile
BMI	Body Mass Index		HGB	hemoglobin
BP	blood pressure		HIPAA	Health Information Portability and Accountability Act
BSE	breast self-examination		HPI	history of present illness
C	Celcius or centigrade		HPV	human papillomavirus
CA	cancer		HSV	herpes simplex virus
CAD	coronary artery disease		HTN	hypertension
CAGE	CAGE questionnaire (alcoholism screening tool)		hx	history
CC	chief complaint		IBW	ideal body weight
CHF	congestive heart failure		ICS	intercostal space
cm	centimeter		JVP	jugular venous pressure
CN	cranial nerve		kg	kilogram
CNM	certified nurse midwife		KOH	potassium hydroxide
CNP	certified nurse practitioner		LGA	large for gestational age
CO	cardiac output		LMP	last menstrual period
COPD	chronic obstructive pulmonary disease		LOC	level of consciousness or loss of consciousness
DDH	developmental dysplasia of the hip		m	meter
dl	deciliter		MAC	mid-arm circumference
DM	diabetes mellitus		MAMC	mid-arm muscle circumference
DPT	diphtheria/pertussis/tetanus (vaccine)		MAP	mean arterial pressure
DTR	deep tendon reflex		MCL	midclavicular line
EDC	expected date of confinement		MD	medical doctor
EDD	expected date of delivery		MDS	Minimum Data Set
EKG	electrocardiograph		mg	milligram
EOM	extraocular muscles		MI	myocardial infarction
ER	emergency room		mm	millimeter
F	Fahrenheit		MMSA	Mini-Mental State Examination
FHT	fetal heart tone		NANDA	North American Nursing Diagnosis Association
GCS	Glasgow Coma Scale			

OD	right eye		SIDS	sudden infant death syndrome
OS	left eye		SOB	shortness of breath
OTC	over the counter (medications)		STD	sexually transmitted disease
OU	both eyes		TB	tuberculosis
PID	pelvic inflammatory disease		TMJ	temporomandibular joint
PIH	pregnancy-induced hypertension		TPR	total peripheral resistance
PMS	premenstrual syndrome		TSE	testicular self-examination
RLQ	right lower quadrant (of abdomen)		TSF	triceps skinfold
ROM	range of motion		URI	upper respiratory infection
ROS	review of systems		UTI	urinary tract infection
Rx	prescription drug			